Social Reading Cultures on BookTube, Bookstagram, and BookTok

This book examines the reading cultures developed by communities of readers and book lovers on BookTube, Bookstagram, and BookTok as an increasingly important influence on contemporary book and literary culture. It explores how the affordances of social media platforms invite readers to participate in social reading communities and engage in creative and curatorial practices that express their identity as readers and book lovers.

The interdisciplinary team of authors argue that by creating new opportunities for readers to engage in social reading practices, bookish social media has elevated the agency and visibility of readers and book consumers within literary culture. It has also reshaped the cultural and economic dynamics of book recommendations by creating a space in which different actors are able to form an identity as mediators of reading culture.

Concise and accessible, this introduction to an increasingly central set of literary practices is essential reading for students and scholars of literature, sociology, media, and cultural studies, as well as teachers and professionals in the book and library industries.

Bronwyn Reddan is a research fellow in the Faculty of Arts and Education at Deakin University, Australia.

Leonie Rutherford is an associate professor in the Faculty of Arts and Education at Deakin University, Australia.

Amy Schoonens is a PhD candidate at the Digital Media Research Centre, Queensland University of Technology, Australia.

Michael Dezuanni is a professor in the Faculty of Creative Industries, Education & Social Justice, School of Communication, Queensland University of Technology, Australia.

Social Reading Cultures on BookTube, Bookstagram, and BookTok

Bronwyn Reddan,
Leonie Rutherford,
Amy Schoonens and
Michael Dezuanni

Routledge
Taylor & Francis Group
LONDON AND NEW YORK

First published 2024
by Routledge
4 Park Square, Milton Park, Abingdon, Oxon OX14 4RN

and by Routledge
605 Third Avenue, New York, NY 10158

Routledge is an imprint of the Taylor & Francis Group, an informa business

© 2024 Bronwyn Reddan, Leonie Rutherford, Amy Schoonens and Michael Dezuanni

The right of Bronwyn Reddan, Leonie Rutherford, Amy Schoonens and Michael Dezuanni to be identified as authors of this work has been asserted in accordance with sections 77 and 78 of the Copyright, Designs and Patents Act 1988.

All rights reserved. No part of this book may be reprinted or reproduced or utilised in any form or by any electronic, mechanical, or other means, now known or hereafter invented, including photocopying and recording, or in any information storage or retrieval system, without permission in writing from the publishers.

Trademark notice: Product or corporate names may be trademarks or registered trademarks, and are used only for identification and explanation without intent to infringe.

British Library Cataloguing-in-Publication Data
A catalogue record for this book is available from the British Library

ISBN: 978-1-032-60323-0 (hbk)
ISBN: 978-1-032-60325-4 (pbk)
ISBN: 978-1-003-45861-6 (ebk)

DOI: 10.4324/9781003458616

Typeset in Times New Roman
by Apex CoVantage, LLC

Contents

List of figures vi
List of tables vii
Acknowledgements viii

Introduction: The social life of books and reading 1

1 Platforms 14

2 Practices 36

3 Power 57

Conclusion: The place of books in digital spaces 79

Bibliography *83*
Index *97*

Figures

2.1 House of Hollow Before and After by Krystal Sutherland on TikTok   41
2.2 Book Flat Lays by C. G. Drews on Bookstagram   44
2.3 Book Poster Shared in Minecraft World *Dogcraft* by StacyPlays on YouTube   51

Tables

1.1 Characteristics of Interview Participants　　　15

Acknowledgements

The idea for this book emerged from a research project examining the ecology of teenage reading habits in Australia. This project, "Discovering a 'Good Read': Cultural Pathways to Reading for Australian Teens in a Digital Age," is funded by the Australian Research Council Linkage Project Scheme (project number: LP180100258) in partnership with Copyright Agency Ltd, Australian Publishers Association Ltd, BookPeople, School Library Association of Victoria, and Australian Library and Information Association Ltd. We are grateful for the support of each of these partners, in particular, the School Library Association of Victoria for regularly inviting us to share our research findings. These invitations led to a conference paper and initial publication developing the ideas that led to this book. An earlier version of Chapter 1 first appeared as Reddan, B. (2022). Social reading cultures on BookTube, Bookstagram, and BookTok. *Synergy, 20*(1). *www.slav.vic.edu.au/index.php/Synergy/article/view/597*. It appears courtesy of the School Library Association of Victoria.

Introduction
The social life of books and reading

Reading is an inherently social practice. It is a dynamic activity that produces meaning shaped by the time and place in which a reader reads. It is also an embodied activity experienced by a living human person who has been taught to read and socialised into habits of reading (Fuller & Rehberg Sedo, 2013; Long, 2003; Pianzola, 2021). To read is to encounter the ideas of other people and the social infrastructure that supports the development of literacy and literary culture (Long, 2003). By the time a reader encounters a book, it has been mediated by a range of agents and agencies as it is transformed from idea to manuscript to finished product. Even the oft-romanticised solitary reader seemingly engaged in a private, contemplative act, a concept Long (2003) critiques as an incomplete understanding of the cultural practice of reading, cannot read without engaging with the social infrastructure of reading. While a reader might not share their reading experience with others, their ability to read and choice to do so is supported by a complex network of institutional processes that produce books, teach reading, and promote literacy (Fuller & Rehberg Sedo, 2013). These processes provide a social frame for reading that influences what types of books are published and reviewed, the cultural value attributed to reading and to different types of literary texts, and expectations about who reads as well as what and how they should read (Long, 2003; Radway, 1991; Thumala Olave, 2020). This book uses Fuller and Rehberg Sedo's (2013) term "the reading industry" to refer to the social and economic structures, agents, and agencies involved in the production of books in the twenty-first century. This framework updates Bourdieu's concept of the literary field to account for the intersecting fields of cultural production that produce contemporary reading culture.

In contemporary Western literary culture, social media is an important part of the reading industry (Murray, 2018; Pianzola, 2021; Thomas, 2020). Digital cultural intermediaries exercise a significant degree of influence on the development of reading cultures and are key figures in the development of digital communities of readers (Davis, 2017; Fuller & Rehberg Sedo, 2023). This short book examines the social reading cultures that have developed on three key social media platforms: YouTube, Instagram, and TikTok. Drawing on

2 Introduction

scholarship identifying a convergence in book and digital culture in the twenty-first century, in particular Birke and Fehrle (2018), Birke (2021, 2023), Murray (2018), and Pressman (2020), we analyse the communities of readers found on BookTube, Bookstagram, and BookTok as a contemporary expression of social reading practices. Birke and Fehrle (2018) argue that the intersection of book culture and digital media is best understood as a process of adaption. They suggest that book and digital culture interact in productive ways that give rise to new media practices that have important continuities with the cultural norms and values of reading culture. One of these practices is the performance of "bookishness," which Birke (2021, 2023) defines as celebration of the identity of being a reader, a person who makes reading and books an important part of their everyday life, and a preference for printed books.

Social media platforms are key sites for the performance of bookishness. Pressman (2020) argues that digital performances of bookishness respond to cultural anxiety about the future of books triggered by media and technology convergence during the emergence of the digital era in the early 2000s. In this context, bookishness is both an identity and an aesthetic strategy that reinscribes the cultural significance of physical books (Pressman, 2020; Rodger, 2019). This book engages with each of these understandings of bookishness in examining bookish social media communities on YouTube, Instagram, and TikTok. We use the term "bookish" to identify social media communities formed around a shared interest in books and reading and analyse how this shared interest reinterprets cultural ideas about books and reading in the new media environment.

While dire predictions of the death of books and reading at the hands of the internet have not come to pass, the digital age has contributed to significant changes in book and literary culture. Thomas (2020) conceptualises these changes as a transformation in the production, dissemination, and reception of literary work produced by the engagement of authors, readers, and the literary industry in social media. Murray (2018) argues that the digital environment has reshaped literary processes including the performance of authorship, the production and marketing of literary works, and the curation and assessment of literary value. The emerging consensus is that the post-digital era is an expansive environment in which digital and analogue book technologies co-exist (Dane & Weber, 2021). This book expands on Murray's (2018) conclusion that reading has become "thoroughly enmeshed with digital culture" (p. 166) as well as observations about the increase in reader power afforded by bookish social media and reading recommendation culture by Thomas (2020) and Fuller and Rehberg Sedo (2023). This approach situates our study in between the macro view of the digital literary sphere mapped by these scholars and the micro focus on the development of book communities on particular social media platforms such as Birke's (2021, 2023) analysis of BookTube as an example of sociable reading practices in the convergent new media landscape and Rodger's (2019) examination of the development of a bookish aesthetic on Pinterest as a strategy that positions reading as a set of practices imbued with social meaning.

This chapter offers a snapshot of two key influences on the contemporary social life of books: the social reading practices associated with celebrity book clubs and convergence in book and digital cultures in the new media environment. It argues that the entanglement of celebrity, commerce, and culture in celebrity book clubs, as well as convergence in book and digital culture, have had a significant influence on the social reading cultures developed in contemporary bookish social media communities.

Social reading and celebrity book clubs

Sociable reading practices have a long history. Scholars examining the history of reading, including Hall (2003), Long (2003), and Rehberg Sedo (2011), have identified a rich tradition of reading communities engaging in shared reading from reading aloud in small groups in pre-literate societies, to literary salons, literary societies, reading societies, and reading groups whose members discuss books in person, to mass media, celebrity, and social media book clubs where booktalk is mediated by technology. Fuller and Rehberg Sedo (2013) conceptualise shared reading as a social process and a social formation with different social dimensions depending on how the social infrastructure of reading is constituted. For example, the popularity of celebrity book clubs has had a significant influence on the development of contemporary social reading cultures. One of the most distinctive features of celebrity book club culture is the focus on the personal reading experience of participants (Collins, 2010; Hall, 2003; Hartley, 2001; Long, 2003). This is an explicitly social model of reading that invites readers to engage with books on their own terms. This model of reading emphasises the role of books as a catalyst for connection with other readers and deemphasises the formal techniques of literary criticism taught in educational institutions.

The celebrity book club model offers a model of engaging with books that challenges the cultural dominance of values associated with the literary establishment. The focus on personal responses elevates emotion as a key criterion for assessing books, while also promoting reading as a therapeutic experience and tool for self-cultivation (Collins, 2010; Driscoll, 2008; Hall, 2003; Kiernan, 2011; Long, 2003). For example, Driscoll (2008) argues that Oprah's Book Club promotes a model of literary value that is female, commercial, and middlebrow, qualities that have been consistently seen as lesser in the literary field. Hall (2003) emphasises the role of Oprah's Book Club as an example of literacy as social practice that invites interrogation of reading motivation beyond the context of school or work. Kiernan's (2011) analysis of the Richard and Judy Book Club identifies the association between book clubs and reader empathy, identification, and emotion as a model of reader response that is traditionally coded as feminine and non-literary.

4 *Introduction*

The association of book clubs with a gendered model of reading as well as anxiety about the relationship between popular and literary culture are important factors in ambivalence towards celebrity literary tastemakers. Branagh-Miscampbell and Marsden (2019) suggest that this ambivalence reflects ongoing cultural disquiet about popular or non-literary reading practices, as well as historical criticism of women's reading tastes. For example, in 2001, Jonathan Franzen questioned Winfrey's literary credentials after he was invited to participate in programming for Oprah's Book Club for his novel *The Corrections*. Franzen disparaged Oprah's Book Club as a commercial initiative for women unable to help him reach his preferred audience of serious male readers (Collins, 2010; Driscoll, 2008). While Franzen's position was criticised as elite and out of touch, similar gatekeeping criticisms were expressed about the literary activities of social media celebrities Zoe Sugg and Kim Kardashian (Branagh-Miscampbell & Marsden, 2019; Marsden, 2018). By contrast, Emma Watson, founder of the feminist book group "Our Shared Shelf" on Goodreads in 2016, was more readily accepted as a literary tastemaker with cultural authority to recommend feminist literature. Ramdarshan Bold (2019) identifies the influence of Watson's identity as a white, educated young woman who achieved celebrity from her work in film, as well as her history of activism on gender equality as important factors in legitimising her cultural authority as a literary tastemaker. Marsden (2018) suggests that Kardashian and Sugg lacked the cultural capital to reinvent themselves as literary intermediaries due to their ascribed celebrity status and association with lowbrow culture including social media and reality television.[1]

Lukewarm critical responses have not been a barrier to the popularity and commercial success of celebrity book clubs. Winfrey successfully established books and reading as part of her brand identity, and her cultural authority as a literary tastemaker translates into increased book sales for the titles she selects (Collins, 2010). Hall (2003) reads Winfrey as an example of Brandt's concept of the "literacy sponsor," which Brandt (1998) defines as an agent who facilitates, controls, or inhibits literacy and gains a benefit from doing so. The model of literacy supported by Winfrey is a narrative of progress that emphasises the transformative power of books, a narrative that Hall (2003) argues promotes her own personal brand as much as it promotes reading. Other examples of celebrity literacy sponsors include Watson, as discussed earlier, and Reese Witherspoon, who has been described as taking over Winfrey's place as "publishing's starriest powerbroker" (Hunt, 2022).

Reese's Book Club, which is run by Witherspoon and her media production company Hello Sunshine, selects books that feature "a woman at the center of the story" (Reese's Book Club, 2023). This goal echoes Winfrey's narrative of progress with a shift in emphasis to the transformative potential of a particular type of literature, namely women-centred stories. Like Winfrey, Witherspoon has incorporated books and reading as a key part of her brand identity and her book club picks "walk the line between literary and commercial" (Grady,

2019). Reese's Book Club also illustrates the close links between contemporary social reading cultures and consumer culture. The website for Reese's Book Club celebrates brand partnerships with Buick and Lavazza as a social bonding opportunity that aligns the identity of brand partners with "a world powered by book joy" (Reese's Book Club, 2023). Hello Sunshine, which was acquired by Candle Media for a reported $900 million in 2021, has optioned the film rights to several books featured in the book club and produced successful television and film adaptions including *Where the Crawdads Sing* (O'Connell, 2022). Brand collaborations as well as an online shop selling lifestyle products and reading boxes that package a selection of "self-care" products with the book club pick of the month associates "book joy" with the curation of an aesthetically pleasing reading life embodying a cosy domesticity.

The Zoella Book Club provides another example of how the celebrity book club model has evolved alongside the transition to new digital media. This book club was founded by Zoe Sugg (Zoella) in partnership with high street retailer W. H. Smith in 2016 and then relaunched as "Zoella & Friends" in 2017. Like an archetypical book club, the Zoella Book Club was formed with the intention of creating a community bound together by a shared reading experience. It had a particular focus on young people and young adult (YA) fiction which reflected the demographic profile of Sugg's social media fan base (Branagh-Miscampbell & Marsden, 2019). However Sugg's status as a vlogger and YouTube personality, and her creation of the Zoella brand as an aspirational lifestyle brand, means that participation in her book club diverged from traditional book club practices focused on discussion of a shared reading experience. Branagh-Miscampbell and Marsden (2019) observed relatively little "discursive online engagement" (p. 426) with book club picks as reader participation focused on visual engagement by sharing pictures of the selected books. The images shared included pictures of point of sale displays in W. H. Smith stores as well as photos of the special edition book covers printed for the club. These visual representations of reading identity emphasise the aesthetic properties of books as desirable consumable goods and position reading as part of an aspirational lifestyle, themes we have analysed elsewhere as key features of "shelfie" (book selfie) practices on Instagram (Dezuanni et al., 2022). Moreover, as Branagh-Miscampbell and Marsden (2019) argue, the legacy of eighteenth- and nineteenth-century artworks depicting women reading in domestic settings looms large over the shelfies posted by Zoella's fans and Sugg's posed images of herself reading.

From blogging to #booktok: Convergence in book and digital cultures

In post-digital book culture, digital tools mediate the social dimensions of reading for many readers. Algorithms direct book content to readers by aggregating data of reader engagement and readers consume book content across multiple digital platforms and channels as well as contributing their own reviews and opinions (Fuller & Rehberg Sedo, 2023; Murray, 2018; Pianzola, 2021). Fuller and Rehberg Sedo (2023) argue that these changes mean that readers are now "more important agents" (p. 8) in the reading industry and that digital opportunities for readers to share their reading and connect with other readers co-exist with digital disadvantages including data harvesting and surveillance, online marketing, and unpaid or underpaid labour. Reader reviews, including Goodreads, blogs, and bookish social media posts, are a key example of how the affective labour of readers is co-opted by publishers and platforms for financial gain (Dane, 2021). As we have discussed elsewhere, bookish influencers expend a considerable amount of labour creating content for and managing their social media accounts (Dezuanni et al., 2022). The online reading recommendation culture conceptualised by Fuller and Rehberg Sedo (2023) depends on this labour, with bookish social media communities functioning as a key source of and site for the performance of reader labour. Each of the chapters in this book investigates a different dimension of this bookish labour: Chapter 1 analyses the ways it is shaped by platform affordances; Chapter 2 explores the creative practices and aesthetic labour of creators; and Chapter 3 examines the power dimensions of reader labour on Goodreads. Both Chapters 2 and 3 consider different elements of the parasocial implications of the performance of relational labour by authors.

One of the most important influences on the development of reading recommendation culture is the phenomenon of book blogging.[2] Book blogs are an example of user-generated media that first become popular in the late 1990s and early 2000s when software such as Blogger allowed people without programming knowledge to publish blogs (Driscoll, 2019; Nelson, 2006). They are, as Driscoll (2019) observes, "intriguing sites of book talk" (p. 280) that provide insight into digital taste making processes and the aesthetic conduct of reading. Driscoll identifies two elements to this aesthetic conduct: "literary discourse" or modes of book talk, and "literary sociability," namely transformation of reading from a private experience to a shared act of communication with other readers (p. 285). In this context, book blogs provide an example of media convergence as a digital blend of diary and life writing, reviewing, and participatory and fan culture (Driscoll, 2019; Jenkins, 2006a). They are part of the reading industry while simultaneously expanding it to include new voices by providing readers with a platform to accumulate cultural authority, or to use Driscoll's (2016) term, "readerly capital", and establish themselves as bookish influencers based on their passion for and knowledge of books (Albrecht, 2017; Fuller & Rehberg Sedo, 2023; Reddan, 2022). The social nature of book blogging culture is further illustrated by Foasberg's (2012) analysis of online reading challenges as shared reading experiences that provide book bloggers with the opportunity to make connections with other bloggers, discuss their reading, and form reading communities.

The reading culture associated with book blogs shares several features with celebrity book club culture. Both promote a social model of reading underpinned by performances of bookishness that emphasis personal and emotional engagement with books and reading as an important part of everyday life. Successful bloggers develop a distinctive voice that expresses their passion about their chosen subject as a marker of identity (Gomez, 2005; Nelson, 2006). The public presentation of a blogger's private reading self requires an intimacy of voice that contributes to the development of a parasocial relationship with their audience. As digital media scholars including Abidin (2018) and Burgess and Green (2018) have observed, the techniques of self-presentation and performance used by influencers, including the cultivation of authentic, celebrity-like persona (Marwick, 2017) and performance of affective (Papacharissi, 2015) and relational labour (Baym, 2018), adapt practices from the traditional entertainment industries and preserve the system of media celebrity. While their comparatively smaller audience allows many book bloggers to have a closer relationship with their audience than celebrities such as Winfrey and Witherspoon, bloggers' passion for reading is, nevertheless, entangled with the commerce of the reading industry. Paid compensation, sponsorship deals, affiliate links, "free" gifts, and professional opportunities are an important part of the economy of book blogging and its digital progeny: bookish social media (Driscoll, 2019; Fuller & Rehberg Sedo, 2023).

The taste cultures of mainstream book blogs, celebrity book clubs, and bookish social media also share a similar position in the cultural hierarchy of digital literary culture. Driscoll (2019) identifies mainstream book blogs, which she defines as blogs that are internationally popular and well known, with features of the "new literary middlebrow" (Driscoll, 2014). Like the commercial literary fiction prominent in Winfrey's and Witherspoon's book clubs, this means that mainstream book blogs tend to focus on books that are emotional, non-academic, earnest, and aimed at a female, middle class audience (Driscoll, 2019). The same is true of many popular bookish social media accounts, raising questions about diversity and representation which we examine in Chapter 3. The connections between book blog and bookish social media taste cultures are not surprising given that, as we discuss further in Chapters 1 and 2, many bookish influencers started publishing content on book blogs before adding one or more social media accounts to their digital repertoire. There is, however, a key difference between book blogs and bookish social media in relation to platform affordances and creator control. Book blogs and the content published on them are owned by individual creators. Foasberg (2012) suggests that this difference means that book blogs are content-focused and decentralised, whereas platform-based social media networks provide more opportunities for social interaction between readers. It also means that bloggers can exercise a greater degree of control over their content as compared to social media users, who are subject to the terms and conditions of the platform they use, including content licensing agreements

8 *Introduction*

and the operation of social media algorithms. We discuss the impact of platform affordances, including algorithmic culture, further in Chapter 1.

Approach and method

Our interest in understanding social media platforms as sites for the performance of bookishness comes from a larger research project investigating the ecology of teenage reading habits in Australia. This project, "Discovering a 'Good Read': Cultural Pathways to Reading for Australian Teens in a Digital Age" (LP180100258) (DAGR project), is an Australian Research Council linkage project conducted by researchers at Australian and New Zealand universities and industry partners representing publishing, bookseller, library agents, and agencies in the Australian reading industry. It uses a cultural economy approach (du Gay & Pryke, 2002) to investigate the cultural, geographic, industry, and economic environments that inform young people's reading preferences and practices. The project is led by Deakin University with researchers from the Digital Media Research Centre at Queensland University of Technology, the Arts Digital Lab at the University of Canterbury, and Edith Cowan University.[3] It is a four-year study (2020–23) mapping the digital and cultural economy of teen reading in Australia, including the role of different cultural intermediaries in connecting teens with books, from librarians, educators, publishers, and booksellers to digital intermediaries and networks. It uses a mixed methods approach to address two research questions: how the sociocultural contexts of teenagers' everyday lives shape their access to information about books and knowledgeable cultural intermediaries; and how the digital ecology shapes young people's reading practices.

In this book we draw on original research conducted in our exploration of the digital ecology of teen reading in the DAGR project to examine social reading cultures in the bookish communities on YouTube, Instagram, and TikTok. This research, which began just as the global COVID-19 pandemic was taking off, expanded from an initial focus on the digital ecology of Australian teenagers to a broader examination of digital reading cultures on YouTube, Instagram, and TikTok. There are multiple reasons this expansion. Firstly, and most importantly, our preliminary analysis of networks of Australian digital intermediaries producing content about YA literature indicated that a desire to connect with other readers as well as reading taste have a more significant impact on the formation of these networks than age or nationality. Secondly, with a few exceptions, it is often difficult to identify the age of content creators or their audience. While YA is often used as a proxy for the reading habits of teens, it is an unreliable one due to the varied reading tastes of young people, not all of whom read or enjoy YA, as well as the number of adults who identify as YA readers (DeRosa, 2017; Kitchener, 2017). Thirdly, our data collection coincided with the rise of #booktok as a popular hashtag on TikTok. We were intrigued by the rapid growth of the BookTok community as well as the extent to which the reading cultures in this community shared similarities with the reading cultures on Bookstagram and BookTube, but developed unique features influenced by the affordances of TikTok.

This book examines the social reading cultures developed by bookish influencers and their audiences on BookTube, Bookstagram, and BookTok. It aims to show how the development of bookish social media communities are shaped by cultural ideas about books and reading and the affordances of social media platforms. It illustrates how digital literacy practices on social media platforms have influenced public discussion of books and reading and provided new places for readers to find their next read, articulate their identity, and make social connections. In doing so, we address the following research questions:

1. How is book culture constituted differently on different social media platforms? In particular, what types of social reading cultures are developed on BookTube, Bookstagram, and BookTok?
2. What emerging practices are prominent on bookish social media and how do bookish influencers use different practices to express their identity and make social connections?
3. How has bookish social media altered the power dynamics between readers, authors, and traditional literary gatekeepers including publishers, booksellers, and critics?

We draw on data collected for the DAGR project to answer these questions. Data was collected between 2020 and 2023 in accordance with ethics approval from university and Australian schools' ethics bodies. This includes qualitative data in the form of depth interviews with publishing and bookselling industry representatives (2020–21) and bookish influencers (2022–23) based in Australia. We also conducted focus groups with secondary school students in three Australian states (New South Wales, Victoria, and Queensland) in 2022. The focus groups were held concurrently with a nationally representative survey asking Australian teenagers aged 11–18 about their reading practices and preferences (DAGR survey).

We also conducted textual and platform analysis of publicly available social media content posted on YouTube, Instagram, and TikTok. We have reflected on the ethics of this method given that the creators of the posts analysed are unlikely to have expected that their content would be included in an academic research project. For this reason, we have determined whether to present research results in an identifiable or non-identifiable form on a case-by-case basis and have excluded any content by creators who appear to be younger than 13. When deciding whether to report on content in a way that identifies the creator, we have considered the following factors: whether the creator is already in the public eye (e.g., is a celebrity, or politician, or has a major public role in regard to reading, such as an author); whether the creator has expressed a desire to share their social media content publicly (e.g., by adding a hashtag to their comment or by participating in media interviews about their bookish social media activities), or whether the creator has provided express permission to use their content (Burkell et al., 2022; Jacobson & Gorea, 2022).

Notes

1 Both Ramdarshan Bold (2019) and Marsden (2018) use Rojek's (2001) typology of celebrity as ascribed, attributed, or achieved.
2 Goodreads, which we discuss further in Chapter 3, is another important influence.
3 For more information about the DAGR project see https://teenreading.net/

Reference list

Abidin, C. (2018). *Internet celebrity: Understanding fame online*. Emerald Publishing.

Albrecht, K. (2017). *Positioning BookTube in the publishing world: An examination of online book reviewing through the field theory* [Master's thesis, Leiden University]. Leiden University student repository. https://hdl.handle.net/1887/52201

Baym, N. K. (2018). *Playing to the crowd: Musicians, audiences, and the intimate work of connection*. New York University Press.

Birke, D. (2021). Social reading? On the rise of a "bookish" reading culture online. *Poetics Today*, *42*(2), 149–172. https://doi.org/10.1215/03335372-8883178

Birke, D. (2023). "Doing" literary reading online: The case of Booktube. In A. Ensslin, J. Round, & B. Thomas (Eds.), *The Routledge companion to literary media* (pp. 468–478). Taylor & Francis Group.

Birke, D., & Fehrle, J. (2018). #booklove: How reading culture is adapted on the internet. *Komparatistik Online*, pp. 60–86. www.komparatistik-online.de/index.php/komparatistik_online/article/view/191

Branagh-Miscampbell, M., & Marsden, S. (2019). "Eating, sleeping, breathing, reading": The Zoella book club and the young woman reader in the 21st century. *Participations: Journal of Audience and Reception Studies*, *16*(1), 412–440. www.participations.org/16-01-20-branagh-miscampbell.pdf

Brandt, D. (1998). Sponsors of Literacy. *College Composition and Communication*, *49*(2), 165–185. https://doi.org/10.2307/358929

Burgess, J., & Green, J. (2018). *YouTube—Online video and participatory culture* (2nd ed.). Polity Press.

Burkell, J., Regan, P. M., & Steeves, V. (2022). Privacy, consent, and confidentiality in social media research. In A. Quan-Haase & L. Sloan (Eds.), *The SAGE handbook of social media research methods* (pp. 715–725). SAGE. https://doi.org/10.4135/9781529782943.n50

Collins, J. (2010). *Bring on the books for everybody: How literary culture became popular culture*. Duke University Press.

Dane, A. (2021). Goodreads reviewers and affective fan labour. In A. Dane & M. Weber (Eds.), *Post-digital book cultures* (pp. 57–79). Monash University Publishing.

Dane, A., & Weber, M. (Eds.). (2021). *Post-digital book cultures*. Monash University Publishing.

Davis, M. (2017). Who are the new gatekeepers? Literary mediation and post-digital publishing. In A. Mannion, M. Weber, & K. Day (Eds.), *Publishing means business: Australian perspectives* (pp. 125–146). Monash University Publishing.

DeRosa, V. P. (2017, June 21). I'm a teenager and I don't like young adult novels. Here's why. *Huffpost*. www.huffpost.com/entry/what-ya-gets-wrong-about-teenagers-from-a-teen_b_594a8e4de4b062254f3a5a94

Dezuanni, M., Reddan, B., Rutherford, L., & Schoonens, A. (2022). Selfies and shelfies on #bookstagram and #booktok—Social media and the mediation of Australian teen reading. *Learning, Media and Technology*, *47*(3), 355–372. https://doi.org/10.1080/17439884.2022.2068575

Driscoll, B. (2008). How Oprah's book club reinvented the woman reader. *Popular Narrative Media*, *1*(2), 139–150. https://doi.org/10.3828/pnm.1.2.3

Driscoll, B. (2014). *The new literary middlebrow: Tastemakers and reading in the twenty-first century*. Palgrave Macmillan.

Driscoll, B. (2016). Readers of popular fiction and emotion online. In K. Gelder (Ed.), *New directions in popular fiction: Genre, distribution, reproduction* (pp. 425–449). Palgrave Macmillan. https://doi.org/10.1057/978-1-137-52346-4_21

Driscoll, B. (2019). Book blogs as tastemakers. *Participations: Journal of Audience and Reception Studies*, *16*(1), 280–305. www.participations.org/16-01-14-driscoll.pdf

du Gay, P., & Pryke, M. (2002). Cultural economy: An introduction. In P. du Gay & M. Pryke. (Eds.), *Cultural economy: Cultural analysis and commercial life* (pp. 1–19). SAGE.

Foasberg, N. M. (2012). Online reading communities: From book clubs to book blogs. *The Journal of Social Media in Society*, *1*(1), 30–53. https://thejsms.org/index.php/JSMS/article/view/3/4

Fuller, D., & Rehberg Sedo, D. (2013). *Reading beyond the book: The social practices of contemporary literary culture*. Routledge. https://doi.org/10.4324/9780203067741

Fuller, D., & Rehberg Sedo, D. (2023). *Reading bestsellers: Recommendation culture and the multimodal reader*. Cambridge University Press. www.cambridge.org/core/elements/reading-bestsellers/8C6D9254C5B8C6DD87714DE3A98CEA77

Gomez, J. (2005). Thinking outside the blog: Navigating the literary blogosphere. *Publishing Research Quarterly*, *21*(3), 3–11.

Grady, C. (2019, September 13). How Reese Witherspoon became the new high priestess of book clubs. *Vox*. www.vox.com/the-highlight/2019/9/13/20802579/reese-witherspoon-reeses-book-club-oprah

Hall, R. M. (2003). The "Oprahfication" of literacy: Reading "Oprah's Book Club." *College English*, *65*(6), 646–667.

Hartley, J. (2001). *Reading groups*. Oxford University Press.

Hunt, E. (2022, December 12). Legally bookish: Reese Witherspoon and the boom in celebrity book clubs. *The Guardian*. www.theguardian.com/books/2022/dec/12/legally-bookish-reese-witherspoon-and-the-boom-in-celebrity-book-clubs

Jacobson, J., & Gorea, I. (2022). Ethics of using social media data in research: Users' views. In A. Quan-Haase & L. Sloan (Eds.), *The SAGE handbook of social media research methods* (pp. 703–714). SAGE Publications. https://doi.org/10.4135/9781529782943.n49

Jenkins, H. (2006a). *Convergence culture: Where old and new media collide*. New York University Press.

Kiernan, A. (2011). The growth of reading groups as a feminine leisure pursuit: Cultural democracy or dumbing down? In D. Rehberg Sedo (Ed.), *Reading communities from salons to cyberspace* (pp. 123–139). Palgrave Macmillan.

Kitchener, C. (2017, December 1). Why so many adults love young-adult literature. *The Atlantic*. www.theatlantic.com/entertainment/archive/2017/12/why-so-many-adults-are-love-young-adult-literature/547334/

Long, E. (2003). *Book clubs: Women and the uses of reading in everyday life*. University of Chicago Press.

Marsden, S. (2018). "I didn't know you could read": Questioning the legitimacy of Kim Kardashian-West's status as a cultural and literary intermediary. *LOGOS: The Journal of the World Book Community*, *29*(2/3), 64–79. https://doi.org/10.1163/18784712-02902008

Marwick, A. E. (2017). Microcelebrity, self-branding, and the internet. *The Blackwell Encyclopedia of Sociology*, 1–3. https://doi.org/10.1002/9781405165518.WBEOS1000

Murray, S. (2018). *The digital literary sphere: Reading, writing, and selling books in the internet era*. JHU Press.

Nelson, M. (2006). The blog phenomenon and the book publishing industry. *Publishing Research Quarterly*, *22*(2), 3–26. https://doi.org/10.1007/S12109-006-0012-6

O'Connell, M. (2022, September 30). Reese Witherspoon and Lauren Neustadter are doing just fine without the boys' club. *The Hollywood Reporter*. www.hollywoodreporter.com/tv/tv-features/reese-witherspoon-lauren-neustadter-hello-sunshine-sale-big-little-lies-1235228211/

Papacharissi, Z. (2015). *Affective publics: Sentiment, technology and politics*. Oxford University Press.

Pianzola, F. (2021). *Digital social reading*. PubPub. https://wip.mitpress.mit.edu/digital-social-reading

Pressman, J. (2020). *Bookishness: Loving books in a digital age*. Columbia University Press.

Radway, J. A. (1991). *Reading the romance: Women, patriarchy, and popular literature*. University of North Carolina Press.

Ramdarshan Bold, M. (2019). Is "everyone welcome"?: Intersectionality, inclusion, and the extension of cultural hierarchies on Emma Watson's feminist book club, "Our shared shelf". *Participations: Journal of Audience and Reception Studies*, *16*(1), 441–472. www.participations.org/16-01-21-ramdarshan.pdf

Reddan, B. (2022). Social reading cultures on BookTube, Bookstagram, and BookTok. *Synergy*, *20*(1). https://slav.vic.edu.au/index.php/Synergy/article/view/597

Reese's Book Club. (2023). *Who we are*. https://reesesbookclub.com/

Rehberg Sedo, D. (Ed.). (2011). *Reading communities from salons to cyberspace*. Palgrave Macmillan. https://doi.org/10.1057/9780230308848

Rodger, N. (2019). From bookshelf porn and shelfies to #bookfacefriday: How readers use Pinterest to promote their bookishness. *Participations: Journal of Audience and Reception Studies*, *16*(1), 473–495. www.participations.org/Volume *16/Issue 1/22.pdf*

Rojek, C. (2001). *Celebrity*. Reaktion Books.

Thomas, B. (2020). *Literature and social media*. Routledge.

Thumala Olave, M. A. (2020). Book love. A cultural sociological interpretation of the attachment to books. *Poetics*, *81*, 101440. https://doi.org/10.1016/J.POETIC.2020.101440

1 Platforms

> It was quite an organic start for me, really. It just came out of a desire to express myself more so than I can on Goodreads . . . the first thing that I explored was book blogs . . . but I soon followed with Instagram when I realised that that was a thing, and it was purely out of a love of it being weirdly fun to take pictures of books, and that community has just grown hugely since I've joined it . . . So it was just a bit of a dominoes effect of finding different platforms and different ways to express things . . . [YouTube] was a bit later, about three years after I started the other platforms. That was because YouTube spiked a bit after blogs, and I was watching a lot of BookTube content, a lot of the big American BookTubers.
> —Nicole (interview, 7 March 2022)

Social media platforms and the readers and who produce and consume book content on them are key players in the contemporary social reading ecosystem. Nicole's account of the origin story of her involvement in bookish social media illustrates a common trajectory for content creators who started experimenting with digital tools as a means of engaging with their passion for books as the digital revolution made these tools more accessible. Nicole is a highly engaged bookish content creator who maintains an active presence on a personal book blog and two social media platforms: Instagram and YouTube. She creates different types of bookish content for each, despite the time commitment involved, because "it is fun" and "I don't particularly enjoy when it's the same content across the same stuff." Nicole's blog is for book reviews and general book discussion posts, her BookTube channel includes content about book acquisition (book hauls) and recent reads (reading wrap-ups), and she uses Bookstagram for sharing and talking about books. While Nicole identifies a sense of community associated with each of the digital platforms she engages with, her interaction with other readers on Bookstagram is a particularly social experience: "It's more of a community conversation-driven thing, Instagram, for me, rather than just the content that I want to share." In emphasising the role of Instagram in facilitating social connection with a bookish community, Nicole illustrates one of the key features of the social reading

DOI: 10.4324/9781003458616-2

cultures developed on bookish social media. This chapter focuses on how bookish social media fosters social connection and community engagement and the role of different platforms in creating digital social reading cultures.

Nicole is one of eight Australian bookish content creators we interviewed as part of the DAGR project in 2022 and 2023. Our aim in conducting these interviews was to develop a deeper understanding of the social dimensions of bookish social media from the perspective of readers who create and consume bookish content.[1] All of the creators we interviewed identify as women and create content in English. Seven have professional ties to the Australian reading industry, with three working in the publishing industry and four working as literacy or library educators in schools. We have used pseudonyms rather than participants' names or social media handles in our discussion to protect their privacy since only one participant has a substantial number of followers on a bookish social media platform; see Table 1.1. Five participants have between 1,000 and 4,000 Instagram followers, two participants have between 5,000 and 11,000 followers, and one has more than 19,000 followers. We have used Instagram as proxy for account size since it is the social media platform used by all participants. The sample size and relatively small audience numbers mean that the examples drawn from these interviews are illustrative

Table 1.1 Characteristics of Interview Participants

Pseudonym	Employment	Bookish platforms	Instagram followers	Interview date
Nicole	Editor	Blog Instagram YouTube	1,000–4,000	7 March 2022
Rachel	Communications director	Instagram Twitter	1000–4000	26 July 2022
Leah	Youth worker	Instagram	5000–11,000	29 August 2022
Kate	Teacher	YouTube Instagram TikTok	1000–4000	31 August 2022
Amanda	English teacher	Instagram	1,000–4,000	14 October 2022
Erin	Teacher librarian	Blog/Website Instagram Facebook Twitter	More than 19,000	17 May 2023
Julie	Library technician	Blog Snapchat Instagram	5,000–11,000	18 May 2023
Victoria	Author	Blog/Website Twitter Facebook Instagram	5,000–11,000	7 June 2023

Note. The number of Instagram followers is correct as of 6 December 2023.

rather than representative. This data offers an important complement to content analysis of bookish social media posts because the perspective of content creators has only recently started to be included in bookish social media scholarship (Fuller & Rehberg Sedo, 2023).

This chapter maps how the affordances of YouTube, Instagram, and TikTok and their respective algorithmic cultures shape how readers engage in social reading practices on each platform. It is informed by two research questions:

1 How do bookish influencers establish social connections with their bookish audiences?
2 What types of social reading cultures are developed on BookTube, Bookstagram, and BookTok?

To answer these questions we draw on data from our interviews as well as content analysis of bookish social media posts examining how bookish influencers participate in social reading communities and express their identity as readers and book lovers. Our aim is to identify common features as well as differences in the social reading cultures developed on BookTube, Bookstagram, and BookTok. In the first instance, our analysis focuses on bookish influencers to understand more about why readers become bookish content creators and how they navigate the affordances of different social media platforms as creators and consumers of bookish content. We also explore how users engage with different types of bookish content by examining the different modes of expression offered by short and long form videos, still images, and text. We argue that the affordances and algorithmic culture of YouTube, Instagram, and TikTok shape how readers engage in social reading practices on BookTube, Bookstagram, and BookTok. The different features of each platform shape the development of different digital social reading cultures with different norms, values, and practices.

From readers to influencers: Digital bookishness and social connection

The consumption of social media content is an increasingly important part of the digital lives of readers. It is a key component of the reading recommendation culture conceptualised by Fuller and Rehberg Sedo (2023), in which readers engage and participate in digital and non-digital networked reading cultures, and an important element of the digital social reading practices examined by Pianzola (2021). As Reddan (2022) has argued elsewhere, the proliferation of social media accounts dedicated to content about books and reading has created a new category of cultural intermediary: bookfluencers or bookish influencers. Bookish influencers are passionate readers who share their enthusiasm for books and reading using digital tools, including blogs and social media platforms, and build a public profile or brand as a reader that they leverage to gain attention and social status (Abidin, 2015; Khamis et al., 2017; Marwick, 2017). They are internet microcelebrities in the sense defined by Senft (2013) although, unlike other categories of influencers, they do not necessarily need to have a large following to exercise cultural authority (Fuller & Rehberg Sedo, 2023; MacTavish, 2021). This chapter draws on Abidin's (2015) definition of influencers as "everyday" or "ordinary" internet users who build a relationship with a "relatively large following" by narrating their personal life and lifestyle and engaging with their followers to give the impression of intimacy based on a "perceived interconnectedness." Similar to the parasocial relationship cultivated by traditional entertainment celebrities, influencers engage in relational labour to develop affective social relationships with their audience that bolsters their status as a trusted source of recommendations (Abidin, 2015; Baym, 2018; Khamis et al., 2017; Marwick, 2017).

The relationship between bookish influencers and their bookish audiences is shaped by the ways in which bookish influencers exercise cultural authority as "expert readers and trusted others" (Fuller & Rehberg Sedo, 2023). This authority depends on influencers maintaining an identity as "authentic," "genuine," and "relatable" book lovers whose knowledge of books depends as much on their reading habits as it does on formal education or qualifications (Albrecht, 2017; Fuller & Rehberg Sedo, 2023; MacTavish, 2021). In doing so, bookish influencers participate in the attention economy of social media entertainment in which authenticity and community are important norms shaping the content and commercial environment (Burgess & Green, 2018; Cunningham & Craig, 2017). Bookish influencers foreground their passion for books as the source of their cultural authority as authentic readers. This representational strategy promotes a personal and emotional model of reading that invites other readers to connect and share their own passion for books. This social model of reading identifies books and reading as a catalyst for social connection in a similar way to celebrity book clubs and book blogs, as we discussed in the introduction to this book. The common feature of each of these bookish communities is an emphasis on personal modes of storytelling that highlight the personality of the bookish influencer as the source of their influence—whether they be a celebrity, blogger, or social media content creator—"[i]t is personalities, not the content, that sells books" (Horton, 2021, p. 46).

Personality also has an important impact on how bookish influencers express their bookishness and on what platforms they choose to engage with digital social reading cultures. The content creators we interviewed identify multiple overlapping motivations for their engagement with bookish social media. While all identify as book lovers and view their bookish social media activities as a way to express this identity, the ways in which they do this are informed by their creative and social temperament as well as changes in platform popularity and affordances. Instagram is the most popular platform in our sample, with all participants posting bookish content on Instagram, and with half identifying their Bookstagram as their primary social media platform. Nicole and Kate post bookish content on BookTube and Bookstagram, with Kate also creating BookTok videos. These platform preferences reflect the demographics of the sample, with all participants identifying as female in the 25–54 age bracket. Erin and Victoria post bookish content on Bookstagram and their own personal websites (which started out as book blogs) as well as moderating a bookish Facebook community. Nicole, Erin, Julie, and Victoria started creating bookish content on personal book blogs before adding Bookstagram and other bookish social media accounts to their digital social reading repertoire. All of these creators use multiple social media platforms to create and consume bookish content including YouTube, Facebook, Snapchat, TikTok, and Twitter.[2]

The desire for social connection with other readers and book lovers is a key source of motivation, with all but one participant reporting that they started their bookish social media accounts to share their passion for books and connect with other readers. Kate, who serendipitously discovered book content on YouTube, changed the focus of her YouTube channel from planning and organisation content to books and reading after BookTube videos inspired her to start reading again. Real life social connections led Leah and Victoria to start creating digital bookish content. Victoria was encouraged by a friend to start a blog to develop an online presence as a fiction writer, whereas a friend who knew of Leah's love of books suggested she check out "all these pretty pictures on Instagram." Another important motivation shared by Erin, Julie, Rachel, and Victoria is advocacy for literacy and reading in general. Erin, Rachel, and Victoria also focus on promoting Australian authors and booksellers. Erin articulates the goal of her involvement in bookish social media as a type of community service that is an "extension" of her work as a teacher librarian. Significantly, this altruistic motivation is shared by participants who work or aspire to work in the reading industry. Each of these participants considered their bookish social media activities as part of their professional identity rather than a separate creative endeavour.

None of the participants we interviewed identified income or monetary gain as a motivation for creating bookish content. Nicole's response to a question about whether she saw her social media activity as a source of income is typical: "[T]here's almost no money in creating money out of book content." Nicole identified two reasons why there is little money to be made by creators who seek to monetise bookish social media content: relatively small audience sizes compared to other types of influencers and the limited budget for promotional activities in the reading industry. While Rachel and Kate reported receiving small amounts of income from their bookish social media activities, the most significant benefit identified by participants was free books, often advance reader copies (ARCs) of new releases from publishers. Another type of benefit identified was professional development or advancement opportunities in the reading industry including book contracts and freelance work such as paid speaking roles. As Fuller and Rehberg Sedo (2023) observe, these types of paid compensation do not offer influencers a stable or ongoing income stream. Moreover, paid content such as content sponsored by publishers or Patreon subscriptions requires explicit acknowledgement to avoid commercialisation undermining an influencer's authority as a cultural mediator. Erin emphasises the risks associated with commercialising of her bookish identity: "I also don't want to do it as a business, because I do want to remain authentic."

Given the relatively low prospect of financial gain, the ability of bookish influencers to leverage the social and cultural capital of their bookish brand to create social bonds with readers is a key motivation as well as an important source of their influence. Bookish influencers use multiple strategies to establish social connections with their followers. Firstly, they present their identities as book lovers by sharing their passion and enthusiasm for books, reading, and bookish culture. As Birke and Fehrle (2018) observe, these performances of bookishness celebrate books and book culture as an integral part of book influencers' lifestyle.[3] In doing so, bookish influencers invite their followers to identify with them as fellow book lovers and aspire to creating their own bookish lifestyle. For example, as we have discussed elsewhere, book "selfies" and "shelfies," in which books stand in for the physical body of the creator, feature prominently on bookish social media accounts on YouTube, Instagram, and TikTok. They function as acts of self-representation, creative displays of curatorial and technical knowledge and skills, and invitations to engage with the social and material dimensions of book culture (Dezuanni et al., 2022). The impact of creators' identification as book lovers on social media is not limited to the digital realm. Amanda's Bookstagram account has helped her make social connections with other readers in real life, including colleagues and friends of friends, since it identifies her as a person with whom they can engage in booktalk.

The second strategy bookish influencers use to deepen a sense of connection with their audience is sharing their own reading tastes and preferences. This may include posting content about their opinions about on different titles, series, and genres, and participating in debate about bookish hot topics such as reading formats (physical books versus e-books and audio books) and industry gossip. Although there is relatively little published research data about what types of content readers seek from bookish social media accounts, Horton's survey of BookTube audience members found that the top two preferred content types were videos focusing on BookTubers' personal reading experiences and preferences such as book recommendations (most popular), and recent reads or monthly wrap-up videos (second most popular) (2021). A similar sentiment was expressed by a self-described "bookish" and "cosy" content creator based in the United Kingdom active on BookTube and Bookstagram: "I come on BookTube to hear people's thoughts about books and so wrap ups are amazing." One of the reasons Amanda created her Bookstagram account was a desire to engage with "sometimes smaller" Bookstagram accounts posting book review content and providing an opportunity to discuss books. Amanda felt that this type of content was missing from larger Bookstagram accounts that featured more posts with "aesthetic pictures" of "gifted books."

Once their bookish identity and personal reading brand is established, bookish influencers use two additional strategies to develop a sense of intimacy, or to use Abidin's (2015) term, "perceived interconnectedness" with their followers. The first of these strategies is sharing news from or about the reading industry such as book cover reveals and publication dates for new releases, as well as creating content about ARCs received from publishers. Posting this type of content, some of which is paid or sponsored, reinforces a bookish influencer's authority as an industry insider. Bookish influencers also share details of their personal lives that allow their audiences to relate to them as people as well as book lovers. As we have previously discussed, this type of audience engagement promotes a sense of intimacy or accessibility that allows an influencers' followers to imagine a social relationship with them as if they know each other in real life (Dezuanni et al., 2022). For example, Erin identifies her most popular Instagram posts as ones that feature her or her children interacting with books: "The most successful posts I do are me holding a book as opposed to just me using an image of a book cover, or even better, my children holding a book." For Erin, the personal element is the reason these types of posts resonant with her audience and she recounted examples of meeting followers who engaged with her as if they were continuing a conversation rather than speaking in person for the first time. Similarly, Julie observes that her Bookstagram account "took off" when she "got brave enough" to start appearing in the Reels (short videos) she was making.

The foregoing discussion illustrates the multiple strategies bookish influencers use to establish their bookish identity and create social and personal connections with their followers. The following sections examine the impact of the affordances of YouTube, Instagram, and TikTok on the way bookish influencers create content and engage with readers.

Branding books as entertainment and cultural capital on BookTube

YouTube is a digital video platform designed to share original content created by users. Since it was launched in 2005, the new media site has evolved from a television alternative supporting the creation of user-generated content into a key player in the social media entertainment space (Cunningham & Craig, 2017; van Dijck, 2013). With 2.5 billion active monthly users, YouTube is the second most used social media platform worldwide, behind only Facebook and its 3 billion users (Kemp, 2023). More than 500 hours of content are uploaded every minute (YouTube, 2022), the majority of which can be classified according to three content types: vlogging (video blogging), gameplay, and style and beauty tutorials (Cunningham & Craig, 2017). While it is classified as a broadcasting site presenting user-generated content according to van Dijck's (2013) typology of social media, the way in which many users engage with content and each other on YouTube is typical of the types of behaviour seen on social networking sites such as Facebook. Similarly, Burgess and Green (2018) argue that YouTube is a site of participatory culture in which value is co-created by users who upload and engage with content and its corporate owner (now Google). They emphasise the embeddedness of cultural values supporting user participation, including "community, openness, and authenticity" (p. 9). Platform affordances encouraging user participation include the ability to rate and share videos as well as subscribe to individual channels and post comments. The absence of a central content producer and programming schedule reduces the visibility of content mediation with search engines and ranking algorithms determining much of the content viewers watch (van Dijck, 2013).

BookTube is the online reading community on YouTube. This community of literary vloggers began to form around a shared love of YA literature as early as 2009, but it was not until 2011–2012 that the popularity of BookTube began to grow exponentially (Perkins, 2017; Scolari et al., 2021). Birke (2023) interprets bookish activity on BookTube as a combination of two long-standing literary practices: the literary review and book club culture. As Birke observes, it is difficult to quantify the number of people involved in BookTube due to the affordances of YouTube. Channels and content are continually uploaded and deleted and the community of BookTubers functions as a "networked knowledge community" (Sorensen & Mara, 2014) rather than a distinct platform or group. BookTube has, nevertheless, established itself as part of the reading industry with publishers regularly collaborating with BookTubers to promote new releases (Tomasena, 2019). Although BookTube channels have a small audience compared to the most popular YouTube channels, several have large numbers of subscribers. Jack Edwards, an English vlogger who rebranded as a BookTuber in 2021, has 1.3 million subscribers on his main channel (@jack_edwards), India-based Helly/Saheli (@thehellyblog) has 583,000 subscribers, and US-based Cindy Pham (@withcindy) has 522,000 subscribers. Spanish- and Portuguese-speaking BookTubers from Latin America also have significant numbers of subscribers (Sampaio & Costa, 2022; Tomasena, 2021), with four Brazilian-based channels and one Mexican-based channel with more than 600,000 subscribers: Bel Rodrigues (968,000), Ler Antes de Morrer (681,000), tatianagfeltrin (620,000), Ler até amanhecer (870,000), and Clau Reads Books (675,000).[4]

BookTubers use several strategies of self-presentation to develop their personal brand as passionate, authentic, and relatable book lovers, a topic we discuss further in Chapter 2. BookTube videos are characterised by a confessional or diary aesthetic, with creators directly addressing to the camera using informal language. They are often recorded in intimate domestic settings, such as the creator's bedroom or other private space within the home (Albrecht, 2017). In offering their opinion on the books they have read, BookTubers emphasise their identity as readers talking about their personal taste rather than as critics or professionals. They offer entertaining conversation about books as knowledgeable bookish friends delighted to share the experience of reading. This is a key aspect of BookTube's appeal because it is the personality of the creator and the way they perform their enthusiasm for books that keeps viewers watching (Birke & Fehrle, 2018; Horton, 2021). For example, BookTuber Cindy Pham, of the YouTube channel *With Cindy*, has developed a distinctive style that uses sarcastic humour to critique popular book trends and comment on #drama in the BookTube community. She does not shy away from expressing controversial opinions and is a polarising figure within the broader bookish social media community. Unlike many bookish influencers, she does not purchase books and her nine-minute video on BookTube consumerism from 2018 titled "why i only own 4 books 📚 a chat on booktube consumerism" has been viewed more than 269,000 times and has an extensive comments feed (Pham, 2018b, October 1). Her most popular videos tend to feature books she did not enjoy reading, and her passionate reaction to these books show how the production of compelling BookTube content does not celebrate all books as worthy of a reader's time. For example, a 24-minute video from 2020 titled "THE WORST BOOKS I READ IN 2019 aka I wasted showering on this???" has more than 420,000 views and 20,000 likes (Pham, 2020a, January 7). We discuss the practices Pham uses to establish her identity as a relatable, passionate book lover and develop parasocial relationships with her followers further in Chapter 2.

The stereotypical BookTuber is a young, white woman (Birke, 2023). Recent years have seen an increase in diversity both in terms of creator identities and the types of books reviewed, with more creators who are people of colour, queer, non-binary, disabled, or neurodiverse. However, the YouTube algorithm does not promote all videos equally, which means that videos created by marginalised creators with smaller follower counts are less visible and must be actively sought out by viewers (Ellis, 2021b). Diversity is also an issue in terms of geography, with most BookTubers and the reading industry itself located in the Global North, particularly in the United States. As a consequence, BookTubers from the Global South often face issues of access, representation, and, in some cases, limits on the ability to monetise their YouTube content. Indo-Caribbean BookTuber Saajid Hosein posted a 16-minute video titled "IS THE BOOK COMMUNITY AMERICAN-CENTRIC?" discussing this in 2021.

The bookish content produced by BookTubers has also changed as the community has grown. Ellis's (2021b) discussion with a group of active BookTubers identified the types of content most popular in the early years of BookTube as "book tags/challenges," responses to creative prompts or questions; "wrap-ups," brief summaries of recent reads; "book hauls," display of book acquisitions; "TBR," discussion of books that are "to be read"; and book discussion videos. While many of these formats are still popular, videos with an emphasis on social reading practices have become increasingly popular in recent years. Examples of this type of content include "read-alongs" and "reading sprints," live reading events in which BookTubers and their audiences read at the same time; "readathons" and "reading challenges," shared goals to read a certain type or number of books during a dedicated period of time, as well as live shows and collaborations with other BookTubers. Other types of perennially popular BookTube videos are "unboxing," opening packages of book purchases, book subscription boxes, or books received from publishers, and "bookshelf tours," discussion of bookshelf organisation and personal book collections (Perkins, 2017; Tolstopyat, 2018). In each of these content types, BookTubers promote social reading practices, both in terms of encouraging booktalk and discussion about reading and in offering opportunities for readers to read together in a fun and relaxed environment.

BookTubers spend significant amounts of time interacting with their fan community and performing "affective" (Papacharissi, 2015) and "relational" (Baym, 2018) labour. The relational and affective labour performed by BookTubers, and indeed other bookish creators, as we discuss further in Chapter 3, includes audience engagement activities that promote feelings of belonging and social connection. For example, a BookTuber might ask questions about what books people are currently reading, respond to comments on their videos, share personal information about their own lives, comment on hot topics or gossip in the BookTube community, and interact with the content posted by other bookish accounts. These types of activities frame videos posted by an individual BookTuber as part of a larger bookish conversation that invites participation in shared reading activities (Birke, 2023). Kate describes this as a feature of BookTube that has evolved over time, with a shift in the reading culture away from performative content presenting a perfectly curated bookish lifestyle to a more community-oriented focus: "I think it's now more a conversation about books, and actually getting involved and getting to know people, and getting to know their tastes and then being able to have that conversation."

While community engagement has long been a feature of the social reading culture on BookTube, the trend towards videos presenting reading as a shared experience is illustrated by the content found on popular Australian BookTube channel, Little Book Owl (175,000 subscribers), run by Catriona Feeney. While Feeney's early content features a mix of book hauls, wrap-ups, tags, reviews, and discussion videos, her more recent videos more explicitly encourage her followers to participate in her reading life; for example, reading vlogs, readathons, and live reading sprints as well as livestreamed reading sessions with live chat and discussion on a Discord server. A 22-minute video posted in November 2020 titled "read with me 🍃 calming nature sounds & music" shows Feeney setting up an outdoors reading space with a camping chair, blanket, and mug of juice during a weekend camping trip. She invites her audience to read with her for 20 minutes "against a backdrop of Australian wildlife and calm music." Feeney's introduction appears as captions at the bottom of the screen rather than spoken dialogue. The rest of the video shows Feeney reading a novel, V. E. Schwab's *The Invisible Life of Addie LaRue* (2020), with a soundtrack of birdsong and instrumental music. It concludes with another phrase in captions "I hope you enjoy our time reading together." The comments section indicate that this aim was achieved, with multiple viewers describing positive reading experiences inspired by the video.

Curating a bookish aesthetic on Bookstagram

Instagram is a mobile social networking app that allows users to upload, edit, and share media including photos and videos. It is one of the most popular social networks globally, with more than 1 billion active users per month, and its rise in popularity displaced blogs as the platform of choice for influencers (Leaver et al., 2020). While Instagram started life as a simple photo-sharing service known for its retro aesthetic and distinctive filters, video now drives an increasing proportion of traffic to the platform. This shift is a direct response to the popularity of Snapchat and TikTok, with Instagram introducing "Stories," time-limited slideshows of videos and photos like Snapchat stories in 2016, and "Reels," short-form videos like TikToks in 2020. The elevation of video content is one of several changes to Instagram's operating model following its acquisition by Meta (then Facebook) in 2012. The introduction of sponsored posts, targeted advertising and in-app shopping have monetised the platform as a significant source of revenue for Meta (Ghaffary & Heath, 2019). Updates to the recommendation algorithm have replaced the default chronological feed with recommendations including content from accounts not followed by users. These changes are part of a strategic reorientation designed to provide users with a cross-platform entertainment experience within the Meta ecosystem (Mosseri, 2021). This means that like YouTube, Instagram is a key player in the social media entertainment economy.

Bookstagram is the bookish community found on Instagram. It is known for a luxurious aesthetic celebrating the materiality of books (Rodger, 2019; Thomas, 2021), which is simultaneously praised for creating a vibrant community of readers (Chittal, 2018) and condemned for fetishising books as aesthetic objects devoid of textual meaning (Kelly, 2018; Rahim, 2019). The bookish Instagram aesthetic is developed in posts that feature beautifully styled books and bookish objects as well as posts that celebrate reading as a desirable activity. These posts are identified by a constellation of hashtags based on the original #bookstagram as well as other words associated with books and reading, such as genre-, title-, and author-specific hashtags, and unique hashtags identifying events or other bookish programming such as book clubs (MacTavish, 2021; Thomas, 2021). Using bookish hashtags allows bookish influencers to categorise their posts and make them discoverable by the Instagram algorithm and other bookish social media users. A common theme is a focus on bookish identity, with #bookstagrammer the most popular variation on #bookstagram.

Like BookTubers, Bookstagrammers spend time engaging with other readers and performing affective and relational labour in their interactions with their followers (Dezuanni et al., 2022). For Nicole, Rachel, Leah, and Amanda the sense of community is a key motivation for their ongoing investment of time and labour in creating Bookstagram content. Moreover, a significant number of bookish hashtags identify bookish communities such as #bookstagramgermany, #bookstagramespaña, and #bookstagrampolska. While the presence of these hashtags offers some indication of the geographic distribution of Bookstagram communities, there is limited research about the demographics of Bookstagrammers or their audiences aside from studies examining the characteristics of particular Bookstagram communities such as Kokko's (2023) masters' thesis examining the Finnish Bookstagram community. Our research suggests that the age, gender, class, and ethnicity profile of Bookstagrammers is similar to that of the stereotypical BookTuber discussed earlier. The creators we interviewed described their Instagram audiences as being similar to them, namely (white) women of about the same age, with two age ranges identified: 20–30 and 30–50. Interestingly, creators reported making more local connections with Australian readers on Instagram than on other social media platforms, with Kate and Nicole describing their BookTube audience as a more international and US-based audience. This suggests that one of the distinctive features of the social reading culture on Bookstagram is the ability to connect with readers located in a similar geographic area.

The visual culture of Instagram, in particular the focus on curating a beautiful aesthetic, is a key influence on how bookish influencers represent their identity as book lovers. Rachel, Leah, Amanda, and Nicole all describe this aesthetic as a key part of the appeal of Bookstagram, with Rachel drawn to "beautiful imagery" while Leah and Amanda enjoy looking at "pretty pictures." As the epigraph to this chapter shows, Nicole takes pleasure in the creative process of taking pictures of books, a sentiment echoed by one of the Bookstagrammers interviewed by Fuller and Rehberg Sedo (2023): "I have a lot of fun making the photos." These preferences are based on the original affordances of Instagram's image plus text format, preferences that also underpin the stereotypical #bookstagram post featuring carefully curated images of books and collections of bookish objects. This visual content is accompanied by text designed to spark a conversation with other readers including short book reviews and discussion questions. Similar to BookTube videos, there are several popular formats for Bookstagram posts including "flat lays," images of books shot from above, often with a collection of bookish props such as candles, hot drinks, and indulgent foods, "TBR piles," collection of books to be read, and "bookstacks" and "book spirals," multiple books displayed in visually pleasing arrangements. Other common types of Bookstagram content, as we discuss further in Chapter 2, emphasise the material and emotional effects of reading. This includes posts featuring objects and scenes associated with reading, the most recognisable being images of bookshelves, "shelfies," as we have previously examined (Dezuanni et al., 2022).

Beautiful aspirational #bookstagram images are an example of the glamourous iconography Marwick (2015) identifies as a crucial element of Instagram's visual lexicon. This iconography reproduces conventional status hierarchies of luxury and celebrity, with images of conspicuous consumption and glamourous selfies designed to attract "likes" and attention. They also share the sensory and sensual pleasures of reading with their followers by posting images that recreate the affective experience of reading (Thomas, 2021). For example, the Bookstagram feed of @myfriendsarefiction (181,000 followers) is populated by an abundance of books, with a particular focus on striking cover art and fantasy-themed props including crowns and swords. The images she posts feature a rich colour palette matching the bookshelves displaying her extensive fantasy fiction collection. A representative example is a post titled "Happy midweek!" (Williams, 2022). Posts by @hayaisreading (146,000 followers) feature beautifully styled interiors that frame reading as part of a "hygge" aesthetic, often with the hashtag #simplethingsmadebeautiful. Her content focuses on reading as part of an aspirational lifestyle; books do not always appear, and when they do, they form part of an assemblage of objects that evoke a cosy domestic scene, such as a 2022 post titled "#QOTD can you guess which movie this is?" (2022). These types of posts invite viewers to imagine themselves reading the books curated by the creator and experiencing their bookish lifestyle (Rodger, 2019). This is a critical ingredient in the development of a social and personal connections between Bookstagrammers and their followers (Dezuanni et al., 2022).

In addition to functioning as displays of aspirational consumption, a carefully curated #bookstagram feed is act of creativity demonstrating the technical skills and aesthetic judgment of the creator (Thomas, 2020). This is illustrated by the Bookstagram feeds of the Australian creators we interviewed, each of which has its own distinctive visual aesthetic, ranging from moody dark academia vibes, vibrant rainbow colours, and nature-inspired greenery, to the clean lines of minimalist images of book covers with neutral backgrounds. In establishing their bookish identity visually, each creator has developed a signature bookish brand representing their take on the Bookstagram aesthetic. This visual brand is also influenced by each creator's response to changes in the affordances of the platform that have shifted Instagram's operating model from one based on connecting with friends and creating communities based on shared interests to an entertainment experience based on the consumption of (video) content (Ghaffary & Heath, 2019). Creators' experience of this shift falls primarily within the first category identified by Arriagada and Ibáñez (2020): change in communication styles. Leah, Kate, Erin, Julie, Victoria, and

Nicole have embraced the shift towards multimodal content by incorporating Stories and Reels into their repertoire of bookish content. These creators have expanded the way they communicate their bookish identity by using a broader range of content types, with selfies and shelfies appearing alongside more explicitly social content such as author interviews and bookish events. Rachel and Amanda have resisted changing their communication style; their content indicates a preference for the original image-based Instagram, with infrequent video posts and a narrower focus on books. Nicole and Leah expressed frustration about the Instagram algorithm, although neither they nor any of the other creators interviewed report joining the "engagement pods," groups of influencers who pledge to share, like, and comment on each other's posts, that O'Meara (2019) argues are a key form of resistance to Instagram's shift from a reverse chronological feed to algorithmic-based feed.

Amplifying emotional responses to reading on BookTok

TikTok, the short-form video sharing app formerly known as Musical.ly, has skyrocketed in popularity since 2020. After reaching the milestone of 1 billion global active monthly users in 2021, TikTok is rapidly increasing its market share while maintaining its position as a platform of choice for teenagers and young adults (Kemp, 2023). Like YouTube and Instagram before it, TikTok has created a new economy of creators, an economy Abidin (2020) argues is marked by acceleration of a shift in the social media attention economy away from aspiration to relatability. As we discuss further in Chapter 3, this shift has been accompanied by a change in the development of parasocial relationships between influencers and their followers, which are now more dependent on the creation of content that tells a personal story rather than the creation of "picture perfect" content (Abidin, 2020, p. 84). One of the contributing factors to this trend is the TikTok algorithm, which ties creator success to the performance of individual posts rather than follower counts. Unlike other social media platforms, in which hashtags play a key role in recommending content, the TikTok algorithm gathers data about individual user preferences including watch times and user interactions (Martens et al., 2022). This means that the TikTok "For You Page" (FYP) shows users a personalised stream of content based on the content they have viewed, liked, reposted, and commented on. Creator popularity does not have a significant influence on the recommendation algorithm, which allows content by any user to go viral. This incentivises TikTok creators to engage with TikTok trends and viral practices rather than spend time cultivating a personal brand (Abidin, 2020).

BookTok is a TikTok subgenre dedicated to videos about books and reading but its influence extends far beyond TikTok. The BookTok effect has had a significant impact on book sales, and unlike BookTube and Bookstagram, this effect was initially concentrated on back-list titles rather than new releases (Stewart, 2021). Many bookstores now have #booktok displays in store and feature lists of books trending on BookTok in their online stores. Booksellers have also credited the popularity of BookTok with sparking a resurgence in reading among young people, with a bookseller from Waterstones in London reporting, "I can't stress how much BookTok sells books. It's driven huge sales of YA and romance books" (Barnett, 2023). However, not all readers use book social media. Our research suggests that less than a third of Australian teens who read turn to book social media, including BookTok, for book recommendations, and that the majority of those who do so are teenage girls aged 16 and older (Rutherford et al., 2024). These findings about the demographics of BookTok users reflect anecdotal observations from booksellers about the types of readers buying BookTok titles: teenage girls and young women (Barnett, 2023; Dexter, 2022). The types of books popular on BookTok reflect this demographic profile, with Ellis's (2021a) analysis of the top 25 most popular videos under the #books and #BookTok hashtags in January 2021 finding a predominance of YA fantasy backlist titles written by white female authors. Concerns about BookTok's lack of diversity echo similar commentary on the BookTube community, with the racial bias of the TikTok algorithm an important contributing factor (McCall, 2022). While diverse BookTok communities certainly exist on the platform, with queer BookTok (Ellis, 2021c) and #BlackBookTok (Sanusi, 2022) notable examples, content by diverse creators is less likely to appear on users' FYP and needs to be actively sought by users.

One of the distinctive affordances of TikTok is video length, which started at 15 seconds, then increased to 60 seconds, and now videos of up to 10 minutes can be uploaded. Despite this change, most BookTok videos are short, with creators making use of the TikTok embedding features that allow use of audio content including popular songs, trending videos, audio memes, sound snippets, and original audio. Users interact with the content of other users by commenting, liking, following, or hashtagging. They can also create new TikToks based on existing content by making a "Duet," which records a new video alongside the original to create two videos in a split screen, or "Stitch," which combines sections of an existing TikTok in a new TikTok. The types of content featured in BookTok are similar to the bookish content posted on BookTube and Bookstagram, with TBR piles or stacks, book cover reveals, discussion of current controversies (#bookdrama), as well as (very short) book reviews and recommendations and commentary on the BookTok community itself (Dezuanni et al., 2022). A brand partnership between TikTok and Penguin Random House means that US and UK users can link to Penguin Random House in their videos (TikTok, 2022). While hashtags have less influence on the TikTok algorithm than on other social media platforms, they are still used by users to categorise their content and connect with the BookTok community (Martens et al., 2022). Popular BookTok hashtags are similar to those used on Instagram, including generic book and reading tags, #BookTok, #bookworm, #bookish, as well as specific tags identifying titles, genres, tropes, and authors, such as #yabooks, #colleenhoover, and #songofachilles (Merga, 2021). Other hashtags identify BookTok communities or types of reading experiences, for example, #DanishBookTok, #sadbooks, #booksthatmademeforgetIwasreading (Martens et al., 2022).

BookTok videos reflect the playful, unrehearsed aesthetic of TikTok. They are short, fast, and loud, most often filmed and viewed in vertical view on a smartphone, with the creator in close-up focus. These features contribute to the establishment of an unfiltered, messy, chaotic aesthetic, which is seen as more "relatable" than the carefully curated high-concept, glossy Instagram aesthetic (Abidin, 2020; Kennedy, 2020; Jerasa & Boffone, 2021). For some bookish influencers the TikTok aesthetic is less intimidating than the filtered perfection expected on Instagram, with short, micro-vlogs requiring less time than creating YouTube content (Jerasa & Boffone, 2021; Wiederhold, 2022). Other bookish influencers prefer not to create video content; Leah finds making videos more time-consuming than creating bookish images, and Kate dislikes the process of adding text and text boxes to TikToks. For the creators we interviewed, their forays into creating BookToks are motivated by social ties as much as the affordances of the platform, with Kate reflecting: "It's not a platform that I see myself pursuing seriously . . . I'm just doing it because it's an interesting platform and I've got some friends on there." However, even if bookish influencers do not use TikTok, they are familiar with BookTok content because it is frequently shared across other social media platforms. Moreover, as we discussed earlier, the introduction of short form video content on Instagram has changed the way bookish influencers and their audiences use that platform.

For the users who do engage with BookTok content, the impact of doing so is significant. Jerasa and Boffone (2021) argue that BookTok is making reading "cool" (p. 222) and creating thriving communities of readers that engage young people in reading by increasing their control, agency, and ownership. Merga (2021) suggests that young readers use BookTok to search for book recommendations and to engage with the experience of reading, including emotional reader responses. The latter type of engagement, affective responses to books, is a particularly notable aspect of the social reading culture on BookTok, and book social media more broadly. In this regard, BookTok amplifies the trend of encouraging affective responses to books in the social reading cultures on BookTube (Birke, 2023) and Bookstagram (Thomas, 2021). This is illustrated by one of the most popular categories of BookToks: videos that show the creator's emotional reaction to reading a particular book. For example, the "books that will make you sob" video posted by @moongirlreads_, Selene Velez, in August 2020 was one of the first viral BookToks to have a measurable impact on book sales (Harris, 2021). As we discuss in Chapter 3, these types of videos created an unexpected demand for backlist titles in 2020 including Madeline Miller's *The Song of Achilles* (2011) and Colleen Hoover's *It Ends with Us* (2016).

The types of books popular on BookTok provide further examples of the importance of emotion and aesthetics in the social reading culture on the platform. YA, fantasy, and romance books dominate the most popular viral BookToks, with the "romantasy" portmanteau an increasingly popular category. As literary agent Adsett observes, these genres of books are designed to make readers *"feel* in a big way" (Seed, n.d., emphasis in original), making them a natural fit for a short reaction videos set to trending music and audio memes. As on BookTube and Bookstagram, the sensory experience of reading is an important feature of BookToks with aesthetically pleasing bookish content a significant trend across all three platforms (Dezuanni et al., 2022; Martens et al., 2022). However, BookTok creators take this one step further with videos explicitly designed to evoke the feel of a book without providing any detail about the plot or characters. An example of this trend is a series of videos titled "convincing you to read books based off/on their aesthetics" created by teen sisters Mireille and Elodie Lee, @alifeofliterature. These videos, the most popular of which featured E. Lockhart's *We Were Liars* (2014) in 2021, have a cinematic feel, with a succession of fleeting images set to a soundtrack of popular music. These bookish montages evoke the sensation of reading the book and are designed to evoke an emotional response, with creator Mireille describing her motivation as: "I want people to feel what I feel" (Harris, 2021).

Conclusion

In examining key features of the social reading cultures on BookTube, Bookstagram, and BookTok, this chapter offers a brief snapshot of how bookish influencers engage with the social reading cultures on three of the most popular platforms for booktalk. Each platform offers a different way to experience bookish social media as well as multiple methods for readers consume bookish content and connect with other readers. The different affordances of YouTube, Instagram, and TikTok shape how bookish influencers seek to create social and personal connections with their followers. BookTube offers the impression of conversation with a knowledgeable bookish friend. Bookstagram evokes the sensory pleasures of reading through curation of beautiful displays of books and bookish objects. BookTok appeals to readers who want to get swept up in emotion.

Notes

1 Each semi-structured narrative interview was conducted using video conferencing software and asked questions about participants' content creation practices and motivation, and their engagement with and knowledge of their audience/s. Participants were recruited through the researchers' own professional networks as well as snowballing referrals. We also invited

teachers and librarians interviewed about teen reading practices for the DAGR project who ran their own bookish social media accounts to participate in an additional interview about their bookish social media activities.
2 All interviews were conducted prior to the rebranding of Twitter as X in July 2023. While three creators reported using Twitter, two indicated that they had largely stopped using the platform following Elon Musk's acquisition of Twitter in October 2022. The third was interviewed before October 2022.
3 While Birke and Fehrle (2018) analyse the performance of bookishness on BookTube, their observations are also applicable to bookish influencers more broadly.
4 These figures were sourced from each YouTuber's respective channel page on 6 December 2023.

Reference list

Abidin, C. (2015). Communicative ♥ intimacies: Influencers and perceived interconnectedness. *Ada: A Journal of Gender, New Media, and Technology*, 8. https://doi.org/10.7264/N3MW2FFG

Abidin, C. (2020). Mapping internet celebrity on TikTok: Exploring attention economies and visibility labours. *Cultural Science Journal*, 12(1), 77–103. https://doi.org/10.5334/CSCI.140

Albrecht, K. (2017). *Positioning BookTube in the publishing world: An examination of online book reviewing through the field theory* [Master's thesis, Leiden University]. Leiden University student repository. https://hdl.handle.net/1887/52201

Arriagada, A., & Ibáñez, F. (2020). "You need at least one picture daily, if not, you're dead": Content creators and platform evolution in the social media ecology. *Social Media + Society*, 6(3), 1–12. https://doi.org/10.1177/2056305120944624

Barnett, B. (2023, August 6). "I can't stress how much BookTok sells": Teen literary influencers swaying publishers. *The Guardian*. www.theguardian.com/books/2023/aug/06/i-cant-stress-how-much-booktok-sells-teen-literary-influencers-swaying-publishers

Baym, N. K. (2018). *Playing to the crowd: Musicians, audiences, and the intimate work of connection*. New York University Press.

Birke, D. (2023). "Doing" literary reading online: The case of Booktube. In A. Ensslin, J. Round, & B. Thomas (Eds.), *The Routledge companion to literary media* (pp. 468–478). Taylor & Francis Group.

Birke, D., & Fehrle, J. (2018). #booklove: How reading culture is adapted on the internet. *Komparatistik Online*, pp. 60–86. www.komparatistik-online.de/index.php/komparatistik_online/article/view/191

Burgess, J., & Green, J. (2018). *YouTube—Online video and participatory culture* (2nd ed.). Polity Press.

Chittal, N. (2018, December 19). Instagram is helping save the indie bookstore. *Vox*. www.vox.com/the-goods/2018/12/19/18146500/independent-bookstores-instagram-social-media-growth

Cunningham, S., & Craig, D. (2017). Being 'really real' on YouTube: Authenticity, community and brand culture in social media entertainment. *Media International Australia*, *164*(1), 71–81. https://doi.org/10.1177/1329878X17709098

Dexter, R. (2022, March 12). The reading renaissance: could the #BookTok bump save publishing? *The Sydney Morning Herald*. www.smh.com.au/

Dezuanni, M., Reddan, B., Rutherford, L., & Schoonens, A. (2022). Selfies and shelfies on #bookstagram and #booktok—Social media and the mediation of Australian teen reading. *Learning, Media and Technology*, *47*(3), 355–372. https://doi.org/10.1080/17439884.2022.2068575

Ellis, D. (2021a, January 6). *The most popular books on TikTok*. BookRiot. https://bookriot.com/most-popular-books-on-tiktok/

Ellis, D. (2021b, May 26). *The past, present, and future of BookTube, according to BookTubers*. BookRiot. https://bookriot.com/booktube-according-to-booktubers/

Ellis, D. (2021c, July 19). *"It's gay and it slaps": TikTok's favorite LGBTQ books*. BookRiot https://bookriot.com/its-gay-and-it-slaps-books/

Feeney, C. [@LittleBookOwl]. (2020). read with me 🐌 calming nature sounds & music [Video]. *YouTube*. www.youtube.com/watch?v=GW3vlvFEC3U

Fuller, D., & Rehberg Sedo, D. (2023). *Reading bestsellers: Recommendation culture and the multimodal reader*. Cambridge University Press. www.cambridge.org/core/elements/reading-bestsellers/8C6D9254C5B8C6DD87714DE3A98CEA77

Ghaffary, S., & Heath, A. (2019, July 27). Why Instagram broke its square [Audio podcast episode]. In *Land of the giants*. Vox. www.vox.com/recode/23274761/facebook-instagram-land-the-giants-mark-zuckerberg-kevin-systrom-ashley-yuki

Harris, E. A. (2021, March 20). How crying on TikTok sells books. *New York Times*. www.nytimes.com.

@hayaisreading. (2022). '#QOTD can you guess which movie this is? [Photograph]. *Instagram*. www.instagram.com/p/CbdGBrZsjRK/

Hoover, C. (2016). *It ends with us*. Atria Books.

Horton, K. (2021). *BookTube and the publishing industry: A study of the commercial relationship between YouTube content creators and publicists* [Unpublished master's thesis]. Curtin University.

Hosein, S. [@booksaremysociallife]. (2021). Is the book community American-centric? [Video]. *YouTube*. www.youtube.com/watch?v=mHNckAuNYvk

Jerasa, S., & Boffone, T. (2021). BookTok 101: TikTok, digital literacies, and out-of-school reading practices. *Journal of Adolescent & Adult Literacy*, *65*(3), 219–226. https://doi.org/10.1002/JAAL.1199

Kelly, H. (2018, October 29). Here's an annoying new Instagram trend: Throwing yourself on a pile of open books. *Vulture*. www.vulture.com/2018/10/the-terrible-instagram-trend-of-piles-of-open-books.html

Kemp, S. (2023, October 19). Digital 2023 October global statshot report. *DataReportal, Meltwater & We Are Social*. https://datareportal.com/reports/digital-2023-october-global-statshot

Kennedy, M. (2020). 'If the rise of the TikTok dance and e-girl aesthetic has taught us anything, it's that teenage girls rule the internet right now': TikTok celebrity, girls and the Coronavirus crisis. *European Journal of Cultural Studies*, *23*(6), 1069–1076. https://doi.org/10.1177/1367549420945341

Khamis, S., Ang, L., & Welling, R. (2017). Self-branding, 'micro-celebrity' and the rise of social media influencers. *Celebrity Studies*, *8*(2), 191–208. https://doi.org/10.1080/19392397.2016.1218292

Kokko, S. (2023). *Encouraging Reading on Social Media. Exploring Finnish Bookstagram Community* [Master's thesis, University of Gothenburg]. GUPEA. https://gupea.ub.gu.se/handle/2077/79256

Leaver, T., Highfield, T., & Abidin, C. (2020). *Instagram: Visual social media cultures*. Polity Press.

Lee, M., & Lee, E. [@alifeofliterature]. (2021). convincing you to read books based off their aesthetics: we were liars by e. lockhart. [Video]. *TikTok*. www.tiktok.com/@alifeofliterature/video/6929091762107469062

Lockhart, E. (2014). *We were liars*. Delacorte Press.

MacTavish, K. (2021). The emerging power of the Bookstagrammer: Reading #bookstagram as a post-digital site of book culture. In A. Dane & M. Weber (Eds.), *Post-digital book cultures* (pp. 80–112). Monash University Publishing.

Martens, M., Balling, G., & Higgason, K. A. (2022). #BookTokMadeMeReadIt: Young adult reading communities across an international, sociotechnical landscape. *Information and Learning Sciences*, *123*(11/12), 705–722. https://doi.org/10.1108/ILS-07-2022-0086

Marwick, A. E. (2015). Instafame: Luxury selfies in the attention economy. *Public Culture*, *27*(75), 137–160. https://doi.org/10.1215/08992363-2798379

Marwick, A. E. (2017). Microcelebrity, self-branding, and the internet. *The Blackwell Encyclopedia of Sociology*, 1–3. https://doi.org/10.1002/9781405165518.WBEOS1000

McCall, T. (2022, November 18). BookTok's racial bias. *New York Magazine: The Cut*. www.thecut.com/2022/11/booktok-racial-bias-tiktok-algorithm.html

Merga, M. K. (2021). How can Booktok on TikTok inform readers' advisory services for young people? *Library & Information Science Research*, *43*(2), 1–10. https://doi.org/10.1016/J.LISR.2021.101091

Miller, M. (2011). *The song of Achilles*. Ecco Press.

Mosseri, A. [@mosseri]. (2021, July 1). We're no longer just a square photo-sharing app [Video]. *Instagram*. www.instagram.com/tv/CQwNfFBJr5A/

O'Meara, V. (2019). Weapons of the chic: Instagram influencer engagement pods as practices of resistance to Instagram platform labor. *Social Media + Society*, *5*(4), 1–11. https://doi.org/10.1177/2056305119879671

Papacharissi, Z. (2015). *Affective publics: Sentiment, technology and politics*. Oxford University Press.

Perkins, K. (2017). The boundaries of BookTube. *Serials Librarian*, *73*(3–4), 352–356. https://doi.org/10.1080/0361526X.2017.1364317

Pham, C. [@withcindy]. (2018b, October 1). Why i only own 4 books 📚 a chat on booktube consumerism. [Video]. *YouTube*. www.youtube.com/watch?v=82aYuS6SNrU

Pham, C. [@withcindy]. (2020a, January 7). The worst books I read in 2019 aka I wasted showering on this??? [Video]. *YouTube*. www.youtube.com/watch?v=L9t8BWltgsg

Pianzola, F. (2021). *Digital social reading*. PubPub. https://wip.mitpress.mit.edu/digital-social-reading

Rahim, Z. (2019, September 25). How the #bookstagram movement has changed the way fiction is marketed, reviewed and read. *The Independent.* www.independent.co.uk/arts-entertainment/books/bookstagram-fiction-books-instagram-publishing-influencers-a9110776.html

Reddan, B. (2022). Social reading cultures on BookTube, Bookstagram, and BookTok. *Synergy, 20*(1). https://slav.vic.edu.au/index.php/Synergy/article/view/597

Rodger, N. (2019). From bookshelf porn and shelfies to #bookfacefriday: How readers use Pinterest to promote their bookishness. *Participations: Journal of Audience and Reception Studies, 16*(1), 473–495. www.participations.org/Volume 16/Issue 1/22.pdf

Rutherford, L., Singleton, A., Reddan, B., Johanson, K., & Dezuanni, M. (2024). *Discovering a good read: Exploring book discovery and reading for pleasure among Australian teens.* Geelong: Deakin University.

Sampaio, I. S. V., & Costa, A. S. (2022). Brazilian BookTubers and the COVID-19 pandemic. *First Monday.* https://doi.org/10.5210/fm.v27i4.12579

Sanusi, T. (2022, April 28). The fight to amplify black stories on BookTok. *Huck.* www.huckmag.com/article/the-fight-to-amplify-black-stories-on-booktok

Schwab, V. E. (2020). *The invisible life of Addie LaRue.* Tor Books.

Scolari, C. A., Fraticelli, D., & Tomasena, J. (2021). A Semio-discursive Analysis of Spanish-Speaking BookTubers. In S. Cunningham & D. Craig (Eds.), *Creator culture: An introduction to global social media entertainment.* New York University Press

Seed, D. (n.d.). BookTok: The next chapter for booklovers. *Contact.* https://stories.uq.edu.au/contact-magazine/2023/booktok-the-next-chapter-for-booklovers/index.html

Senft, T. (2013). Microcelebrity and the branded self. In J. Hartley, J. Burgess, & A. Bruns (Eds.), *A companion to new media dynamics* (pp. 346–354). Wiley-Blackwell.

Sorensen, K., & Mara, A. (2014). BookTubers as a networked knowledge community. In M. Limbu & B. Gurung (Eds.), *Emerging pedagogies in the networked knowledge society: Practices integrating social media and globalization* (pp. 87–99). IGI Global. https://doi.org/10.4018/978-1-4666-4757-2

Stewart, S. (2021, September 3). How TikTok makes backlist books into bestsellers. *Publishers Weekly.* www.publishersweekly.com/pw/by-topic/industry-news/bookselling/article/87304-how-tiktok-makes-backlist-books-into-bestsellers.html

Thomas, B. (2020). *Literature and social media.* Routledge.

Thomas, B. (2021). The #bookstagram: distributed reading in the social media age. *Language Sciences, 84*, 1–10. https://doi.org/10.1016/j.langsci.2021.101358

TikTok. (2022, September 20). *A new way to tap into the #BookTok community.* https://newsroom.tiktok.com/en-us/a-new-way-to-tap-into-the-booktok-community

Tolstopyat, N. (2018). BookTube, book clubs and the brave new world of publishing. *Satura, 1*, 91–96. https://d-nb.info/1243779128/34

Tomasena, J. M. (2019). Negotiating collaborations: BookTubers, The Publishing Industry, and YouTube's Ecosystem. *Social Media + Society*, 1–12. https://doi.org/10.1177/2056305119894004

Tomasena, J. M. (2021). Who are the booktubers? Characteristics of Spanish-language literary video bloggers. *OCNOS, 20*(2), 43–55. https://doi.org/10.18239/OCNOS_2021.20.2.2466

van Dijck, J. (2013). *The culture of connectivity: A critical history of social media*. Oxford Scholarship Online. https://doi.org/10.1093/acprof:oso/9780199970773.001.0001

Velez, S. [@moongirlreads_]. (2020). books that will make you sob [Video]. *TikTok*. www.tiktok.com/@moongirlreads_/video/6858731924865797381

Wiederhold, B. K. (2022). BookTok made me do it: The evolution of reading. *Cyberpsychology, behavior, and social networking, 25*(3), 157–158. https://doi.org/10.1089/CYBER.2022.29240.EDITORIAL

Williams, K. [@myfriendsarefiction]. (2022). Happy midweek! [Photograph]. *Instagram*. www.instagram.com/p/Cbc2Mf8LeY_/

YouTube. (2022, June 22). *Copyright transparency report*. https://storage.googleapis.com/transparencyreport/report-downloads/pdf-report-22_2022-1-1_2022-6-30_en_v1.pdf

2 Practices

> I get my book recommendations off TikTok . . . all my TikToks on my for you page are book recommendations. So I'm looking at books 24/7 on TikTok . . . Sometimes I will search the book, like if I don't know about a book I will search it up to see if it's good, to see if I wanna read it, see if it's like worth the time reading and stuff.
>
> —Chloe (focus group, year 10 student)

Social media is increasingly the first place book lovers begin hunting for their next good read. The way Chloe, who participated in one of the focus groups we conducted with secondary school students in 2022, explains her practice of sourcing book recommendations from TikTok speaks to the broader trend among young people to use social media to determine whether a book "is good," whether they "wanna read it," and whether a book is "worth the time reading." This reflects our discussion in Chapter 1 about the role of social media influencers as tastemakers, but it is also indicative of the role of TikTok as a valued resource for learning about books and a tool for identifying "good" content. By enacting search practices on TikTok to source book recommendations, Chloe identifies the platform as a key element in contemporary reading cultures. Chloe's experience is also indicative of the effectiveness of social reading content on influencing reading choices. This chapter focuses on readers' and authors' digital practices using social media, and the digital practices behind the development of bookish social media content in social reading cultures on YouTube, Instagram, and TikTok.

Practices provide a useful framework for understanding social reading cultures because they allow us to be specific about the socio-material ways in which individuals and communities express themselves and their identities, how readers interact with other people's ideas and work, and how readers and content creators, including authors, make social connections in and around cultural artefacts, including books. Social media practices enable connections between texts, readers, publishers, influencers, and authors to converge online, creating supporting social networks for discussions and creative expression about books. Social networks for reading communities and social

DOI: 10.4324/9781003458616-3

reading cultures are established across platforms, such as YouTube, Instagram, and TikTok, to provide forums for discussing books and reading, to identify the next book to be read, and to establish fan communities. In other words, social media "enable readers to assemble and reach one another faster than ever, they provide ample and readily accessible support for the reading of both digital and print texts" (Dowling, 2019, p. 59). A reader's identity is commonly expressed through these connections by sharing their current reads, their piles of books to be read (TBRs), and their personal libraries and bookshelves (shelfies) (Dezuanni et al., 2022).

Social media enables insights into reading communities and diverse ways to perform reading identities through consistent and recognisable bookish practices. Social reading cultures are identifiable because of common practices both across social media platforms and within individual platforms. The most prominent of these are practices which have evolved from analogue book cultures such as reviewing books, recommending books, and book clubs. Other practices range from the use of digital media to undertake personal engagements and connections with books, to creative practices emphasising the material and emotional effects of reading. Many practices prominent on bookish social media reflect themes that have always been tied to online spaces and are important to readers: identity formation and agency (boyd, 2014; Notley, 2009). Content sharing practices contribute to this sense of identity, as well as autonomy, by offering opportunities for self-expression, identity construction, and affinity with others (Ito et al., 2009; Jenkins, 2006a). Sharing and consuming content about books and reading thus facilitates participants' identity development of bookish personas, and as readers.

This chapter explores digital practices prominent in bookish communities on YouTube, Instagram, and TikTok. It is guided by three research questions:

1. What practices are prominent on particular platforms?
2. How do these practices enable users to make social connections and express their reading identities?
3. What innovative practices do digital platforms enable, including for authors?

Our discussion centres on digital practices surrounding a book's "textual and material dimensions" (Murray, 2020, p. 4) within social reading cultures. Books serve multiple purposes as socio-cultural objects and text (Murray, 2020), and importantly for this chapter, books serve as a "subject (and tool) for connecting readers, authors, influencers, and other [intermediaries]" (Schoonens, forthcoming). Digital practices utilising books thus contribute to the social development of bookish identities enacted through various forms of material book engagement on social media. To explore this further, we focus our analysis on three key themes. Firstly, we discuss the socio-material practices of content creators surrounding the YA novel *House of Hollow* on

TikTok. Engaging with this novel, creators (including the publisher, influencers, and the author) recreate aspects of the book to establish themselves as readers and to connect to book characters. Secondly, we examine the creative labour of Bookstagrammer C. G. Drews. An analysis of Drews's bookish aesthetic on Instagram reveals diverse labours involved with managing her various roles as author, reviewer, and influencer. Lastly, the chapter explores two case studies of bookish performances on YouTube. The first analyses BookTuber "everydayness" and readathons on Cindy Pham's YouTube channel. The second explores innovative pathways into book authorship and reading on digital platforms through an examination of author Stacy Hinojosa's bookcraft practices on YouTube. We argue that practices which celebrate the materiality of books and reading are an integral part of social reading cultures, and that digital social media platforms offer opportunities to reimagine book and reading culture.

Socio-material practices as a tool of social connection on BookTok

Social media content creators, including authors and publishers, commonly perform practices that emphasise books as texts and objects, and embody content and characteristics of the book in question. These physical practices, which some scholars have termed "socio-material" practices (Barad, 2003; Dezuanni, 2020; Gleasure et al., 2017; Hawley, 2022), demonstrate the labour involved in content creation, and indicate the importance of such practices within digital content. As such, practices which celebrate the materiality of books and reading have become an integral part of social reading cultures and a common community practice (Martens et al., 2022; Rodger, 2019; Schoonens, forthcoming; Thomas, 2021). Material practices range from performing the narrative in some way (through cosplay or makeup application), sharing personal reading spaces (including bookshelves), consumption activities (such as purchasing books from bookstores or sharing "book hauls"), curating digital objects that capture the themes or "vibes" of the narrative, to simply handling the book on screen.

Book covers are a crucial element of digital book cultures. They are incorporated into authors' and publishers' promotional campaigns through "cover reveals" (#coverreveal) and performative acts of recreating a book cover through bodily affectations such as makeup, cosplay, and face paint. They are not only important to publishers and marketers, but to readers as well (Thomas, 2020, p. 75). Re-creations of book covers occur through the staging of activities taking place on a book's cover, or through cosplay of individuals featured on a front cover. Where BookTokers (as well as Bookstagrammers and BookTubers) are practicing re-creations, they are offering a form of book recommendation in which the reader aspires to embody the characters or embed themselves in the aesthetics of the book.

House of Hollow *cover re-creations*

House of Hollow by Krystal Sutherland (2021c) inspired many examples of socio-material practices shared with bookish communities across social media. Focusing on TikTok, we discuss how *House of Hollow* book cover practices are performed in various ways by the publisher (Penguin Teen), the author (Krystal Sutherland), and readers on BookTok. *House of Hollow*'s cover features a young woman (main character Iris Hollow) with bloodied flowers lining her face and ants crawling over her. Iris's look is haunted, but she is beautiful. The flowers and her beauty are replicated in many ways by BookTokers through the use of makeup, paints, and fake and real flowers.

The publisher, Penguin Teen, issued a cover reveal challenge across social media platforms as part of the pre-release marketing campaign for *House of Hollow* in July 2020. Penguin Teen's cross-platform social media marketing campaigns have been a long-term strategy, but they gained enormous success on TikTok when a "book domino" video went viral in early 2020 (2020, February 9). The video has accumulated more than 12.6 million views, and Penguin Teen's TikTok account has established itself as a key bookish influencer on the platform. The marketing director at the time credited employee Shannon Spann (now manager of digital marketing at Penguin Random House) with the success of the video and acknowledged that TikTok is "not the place that you go to put your evergreen talking head author video; it's the place you go to live in the moment, do something fun, and maybe be a little bit wacky" (Grochowski, 2020). This commitment to "fun" content is reflected in the publisher's digital practices surrounding *House of Hollow*.

The book cover reveal campaign for *House of Hollow* was initiated in the BookTok video "House of Hollow COVER REVEAL + recreation challenge!" (Penguin Teen, 2020, July 21). Penguin Teen employees make slim bouquets of flowers and glue them on to Spann's face to match the cover of *House of Hollow*. During the process of having glue and flowers applied to her face, Spann (who makes regular appearances in Penguin Teen social media), describes the plot of the book to the viewers via voiceover. The practice of combining short plot description of the book with artistic and fun content reflects the socio-materiality of BookTok content. In the video, there are everyday products scattered around the room such as coffee cups, scissors, cotton tips, and glue, demonstrating how this activity could easily be done at home by viewers. Spann challenges followers to participate in the practice, stating, "If you recreate the cover be sure to tag Penguin Teen so I can see yours too." At the end of the video, Spann's replication of the book cover is revealed, followed by the book cover proper.

The user comments on this BookTok video provide evidence of the influence of the video on readers, with several comments drawing links between the beauty of the recreation and the book, and their intention to read *House of Hollow*. One user comments, "THIS COVER IS BEAUTIFUL. I'm def. going to read this!!" Another states, "IT LOOKS AMAZING IM SO EXCITED

FOR IT" (*sic*). This practice of aligning beauty produced by bodily labours with books and reading ties both practices together as desirable and pleasurable activities. Similar to selfies as a form of self-expression (Senft & Baym, 2015), these practices offer a way to communicate readership and ways for BookTokers to show themselves as readers. To explore this further, we look at BookToker Cait Jacobs's *House of Hollow* videos.

Jacobs, whose TikTok bio states that she "accidentally founded booktok" (n.d.), participates in the cover reveal recreation challenge set by Penguin Teen. Originally a book blogger, Jacobs also has profiles on Instagram, YouTube, Goodreads, Tumblr, Spotify, and Twitter (now X). She also runs a book club on Discord and has become a writer. On TikTok, Jacobs has more than 314,000 followers, and her videos have received over 19 million likes. Jacobs takes up Penguin Teen's challenge to re-create the cover of *House of Hollow* (2020, July 21) using tape and fake flowers draped over her face. She shows her recreation before finally revealing the cover of the book. Like Spann, Jacobs recreated the *House of Hollow* book cover by focusing on the makeup of Iris on the front cover of the physical book (2021, March 7). The video begins with Jacobs holding *House of Hollow* and explaining that she will be putting together makeup and an outfit inspired by the front cover. She explains: "Now, the look we're going to be doing is very simple, just playing off the colors of the covers. And if you hadn't heard of House of Hollow, this book is described as a dark and twisty modern fairy tale. It tells the story of 3 sisters who discover that they're not what they seem. This book is creepy and haunting and I can't wait to read it" (2021, March 7). Jacobs then describes her makeup and application of it throughout the video, commenting on the colour scheme and adding freckles "because the girl on the cover has freckles." The video finishes with Jacobs holding the book in hand asking, "How did I do? Also, will you be picking up House of Hollow?"

The responses to Jacob's video illustrate how the material practices involved in recreating the book's cover encourage consumption of *House of Hollow*. Fellow BookToker Munny (@munny_reads) states, "I love this [emoji]. I can't wait check out the book!!!" Other followers respond to the video with comments such as "This is so creative and you believe i'm [*sic*] picking up this book"; "Makeup and cover is GORGEOUS"; and "I'M SO EXCITED FOR THIS BOOK! Your makeup & outfit is so pretty." These comments tie the makeup application, Jacobs's own looks, and *House of Hollow* together. In this way, the successful application of makeup and its replication of the aesthetics of the book cover promote the desirability of *House of Hollow* as a title BookTokers want to read and potentially own. This practice of combining makeup application with book promotions and recommendations is seen across BookTok among amateur BookTokers and bookish influencers alike. See for example Ayman Chaudhary's (@aymansbooks) *House of Hollow* recommendation video (2021, March 7). Chaudhary's content, which has received over 133,000M likes, regularly includes makeup

Practices 41

application and book discussion crossovers. This socio-material practice demonstrates how bookish influencers utilise their bodies and material objects to recommend books. Practices incorporating bodily performance through socio-materiality are also present in the bookish social media content created by authors active on BookTok.

Krystal Sutherland, author of *House of Hollow*, enacts socio-material practices on her social media accounts on Instagram and TikTok. On Instagram for example, Sutherland (2021b, April 9) engages with makeup application to replicate the *House of Hollow* book cover on TikTok, and like Spann and Jacobs, she recreates the book cover by gluing flowers to her face for an Instagram post (2020, July 21). Sutherland's content indicates that it is increasingly part of an author's work to engage in socio-material practices in social reading cultures. On TikTok, Sutherland engages in cosplay of characters from her book. In a video titled "Are you ready to become a Hollow sister?" (2021a, April 6), Sutherland holds *House of Hollow* in hand and flips through the pages while in ordinary comfortable clothes and no makeup. The video then transitions to Sutherland continuing to hold the book but now, makeup has been applied, and she is dressed in costume featuring elements (such as flowers) from various characters in the book and appears "otherworldly." The transition here suggests that reading *House of Hollow* is a transformative experience that alters the sense of self. Both before and after the transition, the book is held in hand signifying the importance of books to reader identity and to bookish content on social media.

In another video jointly created with Penguin Teen, Sutherland applies makeup and cosplays as the character Vivi from *House of Hollow* (Penguin

Figure 2.1 House of Hollow Before and After by Krystal Sutherland on TikTok

Teen, 2021, May 13). Again, the physical book features prominently in the video by framing the beginning and the end. There are several examples of this practice in bookish content posted on TikTok and Instagram, suggesting the normalcy of the practice for Sutherland as an author engaging with the norms of digital social reading cultures. While much of this content is dedicated to promoting *House of Hollow*, the emphasis is on aesthetics of the book, in particular the beauty of the book's content and characters.

The labour associated with aesthetic performances of bookishness, as Riley et al. (2022) suggest, offers an "optimistic and hopeful affective register that associates work on the body as pleasurable, empowering, and a pathway to self-mastery and being recognised—by oneself and by others—as living a good life" (p. 52). In other words, the socio-material practices involved with embodying the book through makeup application, book cover recreation, and character cosplay are a form of identity performance that associates reading for pleasure with bodily labour. Makeup videos in particular, which were initially created by beauty influencers on YouTube and TikTok, are now a common social-material practice in the BookTok community. Where the body becomes a communicable device, BookTokers perform a kind of "aesthetic labour" (Evans & Riley, 2023) to illustrate the connection between reading and books, pleasure, and beauty.

Aesthetic labours and practices on Bookstagram

Participation in bookish communities, and social reading cultures more broadly, involves a significant amount of labour from a range of actors in the reading industry. Labour is required to participate on all social media platforms, with relational labour (Baym, 2015, 2018), and labours of visibility to gain (and retain) followers (Abidin, 2016, 2020) common examples. Bookish influencers, as we discuss in Chapter 1, also typically engage in labour to develop an aesthetic specific to their bookish identity. Bookish aesthetics (Pressman, 2020; Rodger, 2019) refer to aesthetics that "engage with the physicality of the book" through creative acts (Pressman, 2020, p. 1). The visual culture of Instagram means that the Bookstagram community relies heavily on aesthetics to signify reading and the importance of books. The social reading culture on Bookstagram, as we outline in Chapter 1, connects readers with beautifully staged bookish content featuring book collections, reviews, piles of TBR books, promotional content for upcoming releases, shelfies, and bookstacks, which Pressman (2020) describes as "the bookish version of the selfie" (p. 35).

Rodger (2019) identifies multiple forms of bookish aesthetics that are relevant to the socio-material practices of bookish influencers. Firstly, there is the aesthetic of the book (or book object) itself (p. 475). One of the most prominent practices on BookTube, Bookstagram, and BookTok is to incorporate a physical copy of a book (or collection of books) into social media content. Held in hand, books suggest a readerly identity, and indicate to followers what a video or photographic social media post is about. Secondly, is the aesthetics of the context of where the book exists (such as bookshelves, or cosy atmosphere) (Rodger, 2019, p. 475). Prominent across bookish content on YouTube, Instagram, and TikTok are shelfies that highlight the aesthetic context of books and reading. The sharing of shelfies with fellow readers, Rodger (2019) argues, is a way of asserting legitimacy and establishing oneself as a reader. In addition, shelfies celebrate book love (Thumala Olave, 2020), bookishness (Pressman, 2020), and the book as sacred icon (Dezuanni et al., 2022; Rodger, 2019). As we have previously argued (Dezuanni et al., 2022), shelfies are a practice that invites social and material interaction with books and reading. Through shelfies, readers purposefully engage with and share the material and aesthetic aspects of reading as a self-representational practice to convey readerly identity. This practice is enacted by readers, bookish influencers, authors, and publishers alike. Shelfies, and other visual media conveying bookish aesthetic, are particularly prominent on Instagram due to the platform's promotion of visual identity and aesthetic (Leaver et al., 2020).

C. G. Drews and aesthetic labour practices

Creative labour facilitates the development of bookish identities and aesthetics through the sharing of personal bookshelves, reading spaces, and books, themes we explore through an analysis of the creative labour of Bookstagrammer C. G. Drews. Drews, also known as Paper Fury, is an Australian book reviewer and author operating primarily on Instagram. Pulling content from Twitter/X and TikTok into Instagram, Drews has established a consistent bookish aesthetic across her social media posts. The general aesthetic theme of her Bookstagram feed is one of "cozy reading." She embodies this through shelfies and flat lays, a practice in which objects are carefully arranged around a book with the book centred in the image and photographed from above (Leaver et al., 2020; Zappavigna & Ross, 2022). Such posts are accompanied by hashtags like #cozythings, #bookaesthetic, #readinglife, and #bookish to signify the bookish aesthetics of her content.

Drews's Bookstagram flat lays frequently feature a knitted jumper, hot drinks (such as hot chocolate, tea, and coffee), dried flowers, and tones of brown, cream, and red to suggest warmth and comfort; see Figure 2.2. Books are centred and remain the focus of the image. The aesthetic is maintained across hundreds of posts, though the book featured changes. At times, the format of the book also changes, with posts showing printed and e-books (via iPad or laptop). These format shifts do not alter the visual aesthetic of Drews's posts, emphasising that although books may be read in different ways, the aesthetic of reading remains unchanged for Drews. One of the important features of this aesthetic is a knitted jumper, which is shown in the majority of Drews's

Figure 2.2 Book Flat Lays by C. G. Drews on Bookstagram

shelfie posts on Instagram. While Drews's face is never shown, the jumper, often worn by Drews and conveying the cosy reader aesthetic, is always visible.

As in the flat lays shown in Figure 2.2, books are the focus of Drews's shelfie photographs. Drews is present in shelfies only to hold a book or direct focus to books. This signifies the importance of books to Drews and her followers: they are more important than the bodily "self." However, as Pressman (2020) suggests, shelfies still "serve to project a bookish self-image" (p. 35) and are therefore a practice in constructing bookish identity. The cosy aesthetic is retained when enacting a third digital practice, which is to share content across multiple social media accounts. Drews regularly tweets about books and reading on her Twitter/X account. Drews subsequently captures posts from Twitter/X and overlays them on Instagram flat lay or shelfie posts. In this way, Drews promotes her bookish brand across several social media platforms, all of which adhere to the visual aesthetics of the paperfury Instagram.

Drews has multiple roles in the reading industry: reviewer, bookish influencer, and author. Drews's identity as an author is a key element of her bookish brand with many bookish social media posts featuring her own publications. As we discuss further in Chapter 3, Drews engages in a significant amount of labour to promote her books on social media and has successfully leveraged her profile on bookish social media to create an audience for her creative works. For example, Drews's works feature frequently in shelfies and bookish flat lays on her Bookstagram. This includes a forthcoming novel *Don't Let the Forest In*, and published novels *A Thousand Perfect Notes* (2018), *The Boy Who Steals Houses* (2019), and their translations. Other works featured included the self-published sequels to *The Boy Who Steals Houses*: *The Kings of Nowhere* (2022); and *The House for Lost Things* (2023). The placement of Drews's novels alongside works by other authors foregrounds them as the focus of the photograph, but also functions as a statement about the novels' "right" to be included among other YA texts. This practice helps to establish Drews's own novels as bookshelf-worthy texts and as titles part of the contemporary YA literature canon.

Drews's creative labour, as we discuss further in Chapter 3, illustrates the changing roles of authors, in particular the labour required of them to promote and socially engage with their own books in digital spaces, as well as the work required to sustain relevancy in the book industry and retain followers. The placement of Drews's self-published work alongside popular and well-known YA titles is part of Drews's labour to promote her writing and validate her self-published novels. *The Kings of Nowhere* and *The House for Lost Things* were released in digital format only, and so the texts featured in these photographs are facsimiles of printed texts. In other words, a physical copy has been created for the purpose of displaying it with other bookish items. Drews then applies her cosy reading aesthetic to her own works through mugs, warm colour tones, and the knitted jumper. In this way, the practice of applying bookish aesthetic to digital texts serves to bring them into a world of cosy reading. Further, the legitimacy of the two self-published titles is validated and made accessible to readers through these Bookstagram posts. This aesthetic strategy, particularly in instances when Drews's self-published works are placed alongside other books, including Australian classic texts like *Wings Above Billabong* by Mary Grant Bruce, serves to establish Drews's titles as worthy of a place among Australian fiction to be collected and read (Schoonens, forthcoming).

Performances of passion for books and reading on BookTube

BookTuber Cindy Pham, one of the BookTubers we introduced in Chapter 1, engages with several common BookTube practices that highlight the parasocial relationships between bookish influencers and their followers. *With Cindy*, a YouTube channel launched in 2018, has more than 522,000 subscribers and contains content designed to be watched and experienced "with Cindy." Book and reading related content includes "Read with Cindy" (monthly book reviews), "Friends with Cindy" (book discussions with friends and other BookTubers), "Write with Cindy" (which invites viewers to join Cindy as she writes a novel), and "Drama with Cindy" (videos that address drama, conflict, and trends with the book community), as well as "*A Court of Thorns and Roses* with Cindy" and "*Shadow and Bone* with Cindy" (watch-alongs for the Netflix adaptation of these book series). Pham reads and reviews all types of books from YA novels to literary fiction, memoirs, and non-fiction. The views for her videos range from 10,000 to more than 400,000 views per video. What distinguishes Pham as a BookTuber is her position on book buying and consumerism generally. The books discussed in her videos are generally borrowed from the library rather than purchased. She also has a strict policy for not accepting paid book recommendations and reviews (Pham, n.d.). This means that Pham's success as a BookTuber comes from the passion, originality, and relatability she brings to her YouTube content.

Pham's content is humorous, easy-going, and relatable to everyday readers. Her self-deprecating humour invites viewers to connect with her as a passionate, authentic, and relatable book lover with an ordinary life. For example, many of Pham's videos use the strategies of self-presentation we discussed in Chapter 1 including un-stylised and everyday backdrops such as untidy tables, and unpacked boxes after moving house. She also eats dinner while vlogging and creates content in pyjamas. In other videos, she comments on her personal appearance and health, including references to acne and bowel issues. This practice of incorporating the mundane of daily life into social media content may be referred to as the "everydayness" (Abidin, 2018) of her content. The practice of performing of everydayness allows Pham to forge relationships with her followers by sharing personal experiences with like-minded readers.

Pham regularly engages in relational labour by responding to comments on her BookTube videos and engaging with her followers. Using casual language and vernacular, Pham acknowledges her followers' opinions on books and her content and replies to questions. For example, the "Read with Cindy" video titled "This polygamist thriller book had the worst plot twists I've ever seen" (Pham, 2020b, April 30), has more than 1.1 million views, and has received over 6,000 comments. This video features a review of *The Wives* (2019) by bestselling author Tarryn Fisher, a title that is widely popular on social media and has received high ratings on Amazon. It was nominated for a Goodreads Choice Award in 2020 and reached the New York Times Best Sellers list in 2020. Pham gives the book a 1-star rating and describes the book as a "hot mess" (2020b, April 30). She criticises the work as transphobic and anti-feminist, among other critiques. One commenter sarcastically comments, "We love it when characters/people with mental health issues are labelled as crazy and dangerous! It's very cute and so woke!" to which Pham replies with equal sarcasm, "so cute and quirky!!".

The impact of Pham's review of *The Wives* on readers is evident in user comments on the video. Commenting on Pham's channel in general, one user states, "[H]earing Cindy complain about awful books is such a confidence boost to my writing," to which Pham replies, "I'm glad it inspires you." The direct use of Pham's first name—Cindy—suggests a feeling of proximity and familiarity with the YouTuber, which is characteristic of social reading cultures (Roig-Vila et al., 2021). This type of parasocial interaction is an example of what Abidin (2015) describes as a "perceived interconnectedness" between Pham and her followers based on a perception of intimacy and trust in Pham's "unpopular" opinions and reviews of books. For example, one reader decided to read *The Wives* (Fisher) in order to validate their dislike of it, a sentiment that was based entirely on Pham's description:

> I watched your review and like a year later I was shelving at work (librarian) and I needed to read it just so my hatred of this book was valid as my own. After finishing it a few days ago I must ask: how dare you spare us from some of the worst parts of this book?

Pham responds with a heart emoji. This quote indicates that the reach and influence of Pham's opinions and criticisms are shared by fellow readers. The thousands of comments on this review overwhelmingly agree with Pham and praise her for calling out problematic elements of the book.

Many of Pham's BookTube videos discuss important issues in the reading industry and address topics that are controversial with self-deprecating humour. Pham is fearless in sharing her honest reviews of books and tackling challenging and taboo topics. This is established in one of her earliest videos that discusses an 18+ book subscription box dedicated to the series *A Court of Thorns and Roses* (Maas, 2015). Pham's tone is direct when explaining why she is tackling this topic "cuz I know that nobody on booktube is gonna dare to even talk about it because nobody wants to associate their channel with this mess but guess what? This channel is trash and I have no shame" (2018a, August 16, 0:32). Pham's initial intention for starting *With Cindy* was to do book commentary and make "stupid jokes," but she began to read more critically as her viewership increased (Haupt, 2019). Pham critically addresses books that challenge (or replicate) problematic content and aims to highlight works to influence the diversity of her viewers' readership. One example of how Pham does this is shown in the readathons she has created.

Readathons With Cindy

Readathons (reader-marathons) are a prominent practice on BookTube that provides ways for readers to find new titles to read, find motivation to read, and be educated about books and genres. According to Birke (2023), a readathon is a "specific type of reading challenge where participants commit to reading a particular number of books or pages (or just as much as they can) in a given time span" (p. 477). In addition, readathons, which are a kind of social book club, set readers a particular challenge, such as a particular genre, or set of challenges to complete. The practice of participating in readathons can challenge a reader to reflect on their own reading habits, tastes, and, sometimes, their reading ability.

In 2019, Pham established the Asian Readathon on BookTube (2019a, April 2). It is a month-long readathon in which participants read books by an Asian author, or books that contain Asian characters. The readathon occurs annually during May alongside the Asian American and Pacific Island Heritage Month celebrated in the United States. Pham established the Asian Readathon because she had noticed a large number of readathons on BookTube but none dedicated to Asian books. While the challenge is presented as a celebration of cultural diversity in literature (2019b, April 3), Pham released an April Fools video for the first readathon in 2019 titled "Scarlett Johansson Asian Readathon" as a tongue-in-cheek response to the white actress playing movie roles adapted from Asian literature (2019a, April 2).

Through the readathons, Pham provides "prompts" for participants (that is, other BookTubers and readers) as a guide to engaging with the readathon. These prompts include recommendations, live shows, reviews, and challenges. The challenges might include "read any book written by an Asian author" (2021, April 23, 2:54), "read any book written by an Asian author in your favourite genre" (2021, April 23, 3:17), or read a book with an intersectional Asian character, "because fun fact: we're not just Asian, we are all kinds of different things" (2019b, April 3, 3:13). The challenge is accompanied by book lists that are crowd-sourced through social reading communities using the hashtag #asianreadathon or via the @AsianReadathon Twitter/X account. In this context, the Asian Readathon videos perform an educative function by providing ways for the reading community to diversify the books they read, and to learn about different genres, and styles of writing. For example, the 2023 readathon announcement video opens with the statement: "We are just begging for a crumb of diversity in your reading lists here, so if you can spare that you're good to go" (2023, April 3).

The practices of sharing honest and critical book reviews, and developing readathons and inviting readers to participate, support the development of shared reading practices between Pham and her followers. These practices reflect key elements of the social reading culture on BookTube. Moreover, they illustrate the capacity for digital spaces to influence reading taste and diversify book collections while simultaneously drawing attention to the pleasurable and entertaining aspects of social reading cultures.

Innovative pathways into book authorship on BookTube

In this final section of the chapter we move away from an examination of book-centric social media practices to provide an example of how innovative creative digital practices have become central to some forms of book production and consumption in social reading cultures. We show how creative digital practices associated with digital platforms, including digital games, may disrupt traditional pathways into book authorship and reading. While the focus of this book is on cultures associated with a passion for books, it would be remiss not to recognise the expansive ways that story, narrative, and lore in and around other forms of popular culture and media intersect with books. We explore these issues through a case study of New York Times best-selling author and YouTuber Stacy Hinojosa, also known as StacyPlays. Before turning to children's book authorship, Hinojosa became famous online as a "family friendly" Minecraft YouTuber. Hinojosa is particularly interesting because her creative practice occurs at the nexus of video game play, YouTube creator innovation, and what we refer to as peer pedagogical practices (Dezuanni, 2020). We explore Hinojosa's innovative practices as an instance of how digital platforms enable new ways to create book audiences. Notably, several other high-profile YouTubers have released books through traditional publishing deals, including John Green (*The Fault in Our Stars*, 2012; and *Turtles All the Way Down*, 2017); Zoe Sugg (*Girl Online*, 2014); and Tyler Oakley (*Binge*, 2015). These examples point to the increasingly diverse ways authors become known and build a readership for their books on digital platforms (Sorenson & Mara, 2014; Tomasena, 2019).

Hinojosa (as StacyPlays) first began uploading videos to YouTube in 2014 about the video game Minecraft. The series of videos, called "Dogcraft," made an explicit connection between her real-life pets and the online world she created (StacyPlays, 2014a, March 9–2021, May 16). These videos, known as Let's Play videos, are videos in which a gamer records their own gameplay, whilst simultaneously recording a commentary about their play. The creators subsequently upload these videos to YouTube or another video platform where the videos are viewed for entertainment (Dezuanni, 2020; Burwell & Miller, 2016). Although Let's Plays can be made whilst playing any game, Minecraft emerged during the 2010s as the most popular platform for making this type of YouTube content (Dezuanni, 2020; Hale, 2018). Minecraft is highly adaptable and can be used as an online digital making studio for content about almost anything (Dezuanni, 2018). As a space for creating story worlds it provides huge potential for reaching new audiences, including readers, on YouTube. Let's Play videos are appealing because they promote a relational connection between the Let's Player and their fans, and the videos are popular because of the personality and talent of the YouTuber.

Hinojosa has established her various roles as an innovative YouTuber, children's entertainer, and author in several ways. She distinguishes herself as a "family friendly" Minecraft Let's Player, stating, "I do not use profanity in my videos and do not play games containing offensive language, gun violence or adult themes." Amongst the many hundreds of YouTubers available for children to watch, StacyPlays is a trusted screen presence. Reflecting her reliability, YouTube has chosen to partner with Hinojosa on several occasions, including most recently for #Minecraftyourstory which is a hashtag that is generally applied to videos which invite players to share their story worlds built in Minecraft. In a recent video called "Welcome to Camp Friendly" (Hinojosa, 2023, September 24), Stacy shares stories created by children about their own Minecraft worlds, including several that include original narratives.

As one of the early pioneers of the Let's Play genre, Hinojosa's experimentation with Minecraft as a platform for media production developed innovative ways of connecting with her young fan base. Her YouTube content features a blend of original storytelling on a digital platform and personal connection based on parasocial interaction that has proven to be highly appealing to children. She has created a "perceived interconnectedness" (Abidin, 2015) with her fans by disclosing appropriate personal information about herself, particularly about her real-life pets and her love for animals. In many videos, Stacy talks directly to her young audience and often features fanart sent to her by children. Her videos often feature animal rescue stories and themes, and she explicitly promotes animal welfare. On a technological level, she also experimented with the Minecraft platform itself, by using a special modification of the game that enabled her to introduce new ways to interact with animals in the game. This is highly relevant to Hinojosa's emergence as a children's book author because it established her as a well-known figure in online children's culture, particularly on YouTube. YouTube is the number one digital media platform for children (Ofcom, 2023; Anderson et al., 2023), with YouTube fame translating into other spheres of children's culture, including book culture.

Hinojosa directly combined book culture and her Minecraft play through the development of her *Bookcraft* YouTube series in which she worked with collaborators to recreate Minecraft worlds inspired by well-known and canonical books (Hinojosa, 2014b, October 15). Recreated titles include *Charlotte's Web* by E. B. White, *The Twenty-One Balloons* by William Pène du Bois (Hinojosa, 2014b, October 15), *Island of the Blue Dolphins* by Scott O'Dell (Hinojosa, 2015, August 29), and *Journey to the Center of the Earth* by Jules Verne (Hinojosa, 2020, January 1). Over a series of 70 videos posted from 2014 to 2019 with close to 3 million views in total, Hinojosa sought to encourage children and young people to read. At the end of many episodes, StacyPlays invites viewers to read along with the book and to share images of themselves on Twitter/X holding the book (with their parents' or carers' assistance). In effect, the YouTube videos alongside the Twitter posts act as an online book club where children post their thoughts about the books and commented on each other's posts. Some young people also posted links to videos of their own literary-inspired Minecraft builds. Researchers have since used a similar approach to encourage children to read through the Litcraft project (https://www.lancaster.ac.uk/chronotopic-cartographies/litcraft/).

The *Bookcraft* series exemplifies Hinojosa's explicit goal of educating her young fans about her own passions, particularly animal welfare and reading. Dezuanni (2020) argues that a key attraction of Let's Play videos is that they provide learning opportunities about gameplay, technological skills, and about the topics of focus in the videos, or whatever the Let's Player is providing commentary about. He further suggests the videos provide opportunities for "peer pedagogies" because learning occurs in informal ways and as part of the relationships that form between Let's Players and their fans (Dezuanni, 2020). For many fans, these relationships resemble parasocial friendships in which fans feel they have a personal connection to the YouTuber. Hinojosa's five books, written under her online celebrity name StacyPlays, include the four books of the *Wild Rescuers* series published between 2018 and 2021; and the first book of the *Rescue Tails* series, published in 2024. All five books are based in the same story world and based on characters that originate in Stacy's Minecraft videos, particularly *Dogcraft*. The books feature a young girl, Stacy, who has been raised by wolves and are promoted as a "Minecraft inspired fantasy adventure series" (Amazon, n.d.). Within the *Dogcraft* YouTube series, Hinojosa demonstrates innovative ways for YouTuber-authors to promote their published works. Posters for her book series *Wild Rescuers* (2018–), and *Rescue Tails* (2024–), appear in the world of *Dogcraft*. Figure 2.3 is a screenshot from the most recent *Dogcraft* video (Hinojosa, 2021a), which shows a poster for Hinojosa's book *Sentinels in the Deep Ocean* (2021b).

In this video, the camera view pulls back so that viewers can see the poster in full and absorb its contents. A caption on the poster states "Creator of the YouTube series Dogcraft." The poster functions as a promotional technique that combines Hinojosa's roles as YouTuber, author, and Minecraft gameplayer. This example demonstrates the evolving and adaptable roles of authors participating in social reading cultures, as with the Drews and Sutherland case studies discussed earlier in this chapter.

Hinojosa's innovative pathway into children's book authorship, and the consequent development of her fanbase of readers is indicative of how book-related practices on digital platforms such as YouTube and Minecraft have disrupted traditional pathways into authorship and reading. The StacyPlays authored novels sit somewhere between traditional novels and so-called AFK

Figure 2.3 Book Poster Shared in Minecraft World *Dogcraft* by StacyPlays on YouTube

(away from keyboard) books, which typically expand games-based story-worlds. The rich narratives available within video games have long been the basis for the kinds of fan-based practices and labour described earlier in the chapter, leading to the formation of online communities, forms of social interaction (Milner, 2009), and peer pedagogies (Dezuanni, 2020).

In the overall examination of digital practices associated with books and reading, it is important to recognise that many readers of books consume and play narratives and story-worlds online and within games first. More broadly, the digital practices performed by creators and fans associated with stories, narrative, and lore may or may not intersect with books and the reading industry. Authors such as StacyPlays have used digital platforms to bridge the gap between online story-worlds and traditional publishing. As a pioneer of the Let's Play genre, Hinojosa has used Minecraft to create a rich fictional world. She has also undertaken a great deal of relational labour to build her viewership (and eventual readership), through posting regularly to YouTube and other social media platforms. In turn, her fans have undertaken their own practices to build community around both her Minecraft world and novels.

Conclusion

In this chapter we have discussed several of the digital practices connected with social reading cultures. We have shown how practices on BookTok emphasise the material aspects of books and reading, and how these practices are enacted by many different actors in the reading industry, including readers, authors, and publishers. Analysis of Drews's Bookstagram account demonstrated how aesthetic labour contributes to the reading identity of Bookstagrammers and offers new ways for authors to promote and share their own publications. We also examined two different models of social reading practices on YouTube. Firstly, our case study of Pham's *With Cindy* Book-Tube content provided insight into how bookish influencers develop parasocial relationships with followers through performances of relatability and everydayness. As part of our discussion on YouTube, we also explored the innovative digital practices of YouTuber-turned-author StacyPlays, who combined her passion for books and reading with the video game Minecraft in Let's Play YouTube content.

Reference list

Abidin, C. (2015). Communicative ♥ intimacies: Influencers and perceived interconnectedness. *Ada: A Journal of Gender, New Media, and Technology, 8*. https://doi.org/10.7264/N3MW2FFG

Abidin, C. (2016). Visibility labour: Engaging with Influencers' fashion brands and #OOTD advertorial campaigns on Instagram. *Media International Australia, 161*(1), 86–100. https://doi.org/10.1177/1329878X16665177

Abidin, C. (2018). *Internet celebrity: Understanding fame online*. Emerald Publishing.

Abidin, C. (2020). Mapping internet celebrity on TikTok: Exploring attention economies and visibility labours. *Cultural Science Journal*, *12*(1), 77–103. http://doi.org/10.5334/csci.140

Amazon (n.d.). *Wild rescuers* (4 book series). Retrieved December 14, 2023, from www.amazon.com/Wild-Rescuers-4-book-series/dp/B07KY4VGMF

Anderson, M., Faverio, M. & Gottfried, J. (2023). Teens, social media and technology 2023. *Pew Research Centre*. www.pewresearch.org/internet/wp-content/uploads/sites/9/2023/12/PI_2023.12.11-Teens-Social-Media-Tech_FINAL.pdf

Barad, K. (2003). Posthumanist performativity: Toward an understanding of how matter comes to matter. *Signs: Journal of Women in Culture and Society*, *28*(3), 801–831. https://doi.org/10.1086/345321

Baym, N. K. (2015). Connect with your audience! The relational labor of connection. *The Communication Review*, *18*(1), 14–22. https://doi.org/10.1080/10714421.2015.996401

Baym, N. K. (2018). *Playing to the crowd: Musicians, audiences, and the intimate work of connection*. New York University Press. https://doi.org/10.2307/j.ctv12pnpcg

Birke, D. (2023). "Doing" literary reading online: The case of Booktube. In A. Ensslin, J. Round, & B. Thomas (Eds.), *The Routledge companion to literary media* (pp. 468–478). Taylor & Francis Group.

boyd, d. (2014). *It's complicated: The social lives of networked teens*. Yale University Press.

Burwell, C., & Miller, T. (2016). Let's play: Exploring literacy practices in an emerging videogame paratext. *E-Learning and Digital Media*, *13*(3–4), 109–125.

Chaudhary, A. [@aymansbooks]. (2021, March 7). *@penguin_teen CHECK OUT #HouseofHollow #PenguinTeenPartner #PenguinTEen #bookrec #booktok* [Video]. TikTok. https://www.tiktok.com/@aymansbooks/video/6936600453106978054

Dezuanni, M. (2018). Minecraft and children's digital making: Implications for media literacy education. *Learning, Media and Technology*, *43*(3), 236–249. https://doi.org/10.1080/17439884.2018.1472607

Dezuanni, M. (2020). *Peer pedagogies: Learning with Minecraft let's play videos*. The MIT Press.

Dezuanni, M., Reddan, B., Rutherford, L., & Schoonens, A. (2022). Selfies and shelfies on #bookstagram and #booktok–social media and the mediation of Australian teen reading. *Learning, Media and Technology*, *47*(3), 355–372. https://doi.org/10.1080/17439884.2022.2068575

Dowling, D. (2019). *Immersive longform storytelling: Media, technology, audience*. Routledge.

Drews, C. G. (2019). *The boy who steals houses*. Orchard Books.

Drews, C. G. [@Paperfury]. (ca. 2022). *The kings of nowhere*. Patreon.

Evans, A., & Riley, S. (2023). *Digital feeling*. Palgrave Macmillan.

Fisher, T. (2019). *The wives*. Graydon House.

Gleasure, R., O'Reilly, P., & Cahalane, M. (2017). Inclusive technologies, selective traditions: A socio-material case study of crowdfunded book publishing. *Journal of Information Technology*, *32*, 326–343. https://doi.org/10.1057/s41265-017-0041-y

Grant Bruce, M. (1935). *Wings above Billabong*. Ward, Lock.

54 Practices

Green, J. (2012). *The fault in our stars*. Penguin.
Green, J. (2017). *Turtles all the way down*. Penguin.
Grochowski, S. (2020, March 5). PenguinTeen finds success on TikTok with viral video. *Publishers Weekly*. www.publishersweekly.com/pw/by-topic/childrens/childrens-industry-news/article/82611-penguinteen-finds-success-on-tiktok-with-viral-video.html
Hale, J. L. (2018, September 19). 'Fortnite is not YouTube's most popular game. *Tubefilter*. www.tubefilter.com/2018/09/19/fortnite-is-not-youtubes-most-popular-game/
Haupt, A. (2019, August 6). The Bookstagrammers and BookTubers changing the way we read. *The Washington Post*. www.washingtonpost.com/entertainment/books/the-bookstagrammers-and-booktubers-changing-the-way-we-read/2019/08/06/60b76d6a-afb6-11e9-8e77-03b30bc29f64_story.html
Hawley, S. (2022). Doing sociomaterial studies: The circuit of agency. *Learning Media and Technology*, *47*(4), 413–426. https://doi.org/10.1080/17439884.2021.1986064
Hinojosa, S. [@stacyplays]. (2014a, March 9–2021, May 16). Dogcraft. [Video series]. *YouTube*. www.youtube.com/playlist?list=PLc5xWgIisSO3CYeJFSzAX5fali9K_Uxwy
Hinojosa, S. [@stacyplays]. (2014b, October 15). The first book! Bookcraft (Ep. 3). [Video]. *YouTube*. www.youtube.com/watch?v=tFidJQ2ilug
Hinojosa, S. [@stacyplays]. (2015, August 29). Island of the blue dolphins: Bookcraft (CH.61). [Video]. *YouTube*. www.youtube.com/watch?v=PFihZUWV2_c
Hinojosa, S. [StacyPlays]. (2018–). *Wild rescuers series*. HarperCollins.
Hinojosa, S. [@stacyplays]. (2020, January 1). *Journey to the centre of the Earth: Bookcraft*. [Video]. *YouTube*. www.youtube.com/watch?v=OGiU2H4NUhA
Hinojosa, S. [@stacyplays]. (2021a, May 16). Page's rainbow bridge: Dogcraft (Ep. 342). [Video]. *YouTube*. www.youtube.com/watch?v=jcARqP8rW1Y
Hinojosa, S. [StacyPlays]. (2021b). *Sentinels in the deep ocean*. HarperCollins.
Hinojosa, S. [@stacyplays]. (2023, September 24). Welcome to Camp Friendly! #Minecraftyourstory. [Video]. *YouTube*. www.youtube.com/watch?v=0bKhili6t9Y
Hinojosa, S. [StacyPlays]. (2024–). *Rescue tails*. HarperCollins.
Ito, M., Baumer, S., Bittanti, M., boyd, d., Cody, R., Herr-Stephenson, B., & Tripp, L. (2009). *Hanging out, messing around, and geeking out: Kids living and learning with new media*. The MIT Press.
Jacobs, C. [@caitsbooks]. (2020, July 21). Go check out @penguin_teen to learn more about this book! #houseofHollow #booktok #coverreveal #fyp #books [Video]. *TikTok*. www.tiktok.com/@caitsbooks/video/6851593415046581510
Jacobs, C. [@caitsbooks]. (2021, March 7). This just made me realize that i need more floral stuff @penguin_teen #HouseofHollow (sic). [Video]. *TikTok*. www.tiktok.com/@caitsbooks/video/6936572647119572230
Jacobs, C. [@caitsbooks]. (n.d.). [TikTok Profile]. *TikTok*. Retrieved December 21, 2023, from www.tiktok.com/@caitsbooks
Jenkins, H. (2006a). *Convergence culture: Where old and new media collide*. New York University Press.

Leaver, T., Highfield, T., & Abidin, C. (2020). *Instagram: Visual social media cultures*. Polity Press.

Maas, S. J. (2015). *A court of thorns and roses*. Bloomsbury.

Martens, M., Balling, G., & Higgason, K. A. (2022). #BookTokMadeMeReadIt: Young adult reading communities across an international, sociotechnical landscape. *Information and Learning Sciences*, *123*(11/12), 705–722. https://doi.org/10.1108/ILS-07-2022-0086

Milner, R. M. (2009). Working for the text: Fan labor and the new organization. *International Journal of Cultural Studies*, *12*(5), 491–508. https://doi.org/10.1177/1367877909337861

Murray, S. (2020). *Introduction to contemporary print culture: Books as media*. Taylor & Francis.

Notley, T. (2009). Young people, online networks, and social inclusion. *Journal of Computer-Mediated Communication*, *14*(4), 1208–1227. https://doi.org/10.1111/j.1083-6101.2009.01487x

Oakley, T. (2015). *Binge*. Simon & Schuster.

Ofcom. (2023). *Children's media lives 2023: A report for Ofcom*. www.ofcom.org.uk/__data/assets/pdf_file/0025/255850/childrens-media-lives-2023-summary-report.pdf

Penguin Teen [@penguin_teen]. (2020a, July 21). House of Hollow COVER REVEAL + recreation challenge! #booktok #books #houseofhollow #krystalsutherland. [Video]. *TikTok*. www.tiktok.com/@penguin_teen/video/6851594184055409926

Penguin Teen [@penguin_teen]. (2020b, February 9). Pls don't let this flop it's a miracle i still have a job #foryou #fyp #fy #dominos #books #officelife #viral (sic). [Video]. *TikTok*. www.tiktok.com/@penguin_teen/video/6791228381066169606?q=%22book%20domino%22%20%23penguinteen%202020&t=1702724064281

Penguin Teen [@penguin_teen]. (2021, May 13). The #unsolved case of the Somerton man + some epic Vivi cosplay from #HouseofHollow author @krystal_sutherland! #booktok [Video]. *TikTok*. www.tiktok.com/@penguin_teen/video/6961514637280038149

Pham, C. [@withcindy]. (2018a, August 16). Unboxing soap gate. [Video]. *YouTube*. www.youtube.com/watch?v=iaj-UO5X2RQ&

Pham, C. [@withcindy]. (2019a, April 2). Scarlett Johansson Asian Readathon. [Video]. *YouTube*. www.youtube.com/watch?v=ACvS_ckjIYw

Pham, C. [@withcindy]. (2019b, April 3). Asian Readathon—May 2019. [Video]. *YouTube*. www.youtube.com/watch?v=ODMHgqII52c

Pham, C. [@withcindy]. (2020b, April 30). This polygamist thriller book had the worst plot twists I've ever seen . . . [Video]. *YouTube*. www.youtube.com/watch?v=wE5n7auyLs0

Pham, C. [@withcindy]. (2021, April 23). 2021 Asian Readathon [Video]. *YouTube*. https://www.youtube.com/watch?v=wxxOc_rW8go&list=PLfDByaG5ml_7STlC-26AMZq1UMtU3HaRb

Pham, C. [@withcindy]. (2023, April 5). 2023 Asian readathon announcement [Video]. *YouTube*. https://www.youtube.com/watch?v=CtkQuu3K69w

Pham, C. (n.d.). *FAQs. With Cindy*. https://withcindy.carrd.co/#faq

Pressman, J. (2020). *Bookishness: Loving books in a digital age*. Columbia University Press.
Riley, S., Evans, A., & Robson, M. (2022). *Postfeminism and body image*. Routledge.
Rodger, N. (2019). From bookshelf porn and shelfies to #bookfacefriday: How readers use Pinterest to promote their bookishness. *Participations: Journal of Audience and Reception Studies*, *16*(1), 473–495.
Roig-Vila, R., Romero-Guerra, H., & Rovira-Collado, J. (2021). BookTubers as multimodal reading influencers: An analysis of subscriber interactions. *Multimodal Technologies and Interaction*, *5*(7), 39. https://doi.org/10.3390/mti5070039
Schoonens, A. (forthcoming). *Exploring digital media ecologies of young adult fiction: Teen readers and online participatory cultures* [Doctoral dissertation, Queensland University of Technology].
Senft, T. M., & Baym, N. K. (2015). What does the selfie say? Investigating a global phenomenon. *International Journal of Communication*, *9*, 1588–1606.
Sorenson, K., & Mara, A. (2014). BookTubers as a networked knowledge community. In M. Limbu & B. Gurung (Eds), *Emerging pedagogies in the networked knowledge society: Practices integrating social media and globalization* (pp. 87–99). Information Science Reference.
Sugg, Z. (2014). *Girl online*. Atria/Keywords Press.
Sutherland, K. [@km_sutherland]. (2020, July 21). 🐍 🕷 COVER REVEAL! 🕷 🐍 most of the time, author life involves hour after hour of staring at a screen. [Photograph]. *Instagram*. www.instagram.com/p/CC3rOU3AoZu
Sutherland, K. [@krystal_sutherland]. (2021a, April 6). Are you ready to become a Hollow sister? Show me your #houseofhollow before and after! #booktok #reading. #fyp #foryou. [Video]. *TikTok*. www.tiktok.com/@krystal_sutherland/video/6948009387860577541
Sutherland, K. [@krystal_sutherland]. (2021b, April 9). Before and after Reneé Ahdieh's House of Hollow makeup tutorial ♥ #houseofhollow #reneeahdieh#thewrathandthedawn #fyp #foryou. [Video]. *TikTok*. www.tiktok.com/@krystal_sutherland/video/6948892289532005637
Sutherland, K. (2021c). *House of hollow*. Penguin Books.
Thomas, B. (2020). *Literature and social media*. Routledge.
Thomas, B. (2021). The #bookstagram: distributed reading in the social media age. *Language Sciences*, *84*, 1–10. https://doi.org/10.1016/j.langsci.2021.101358
Thumala Olave, M. A. (2020). Book love: A cultural sociological interpretation of the attachment to books. *Poetics*, *81*, 101440. https://doi.org/10.1016/j.poetic.2020.1010440
Tomasena, J. (2019). Negotiating collaborations: BookTubers, the publishing industry, and YouTube's ecosystem. *Social Media + Society*, *5*(4), 1–12. https://doi.org/10.1177/2056305119894004
Zappavigna, M., & Ross, A. S. (2022). Instagram and intermodal configurations of value: Ideology, aesthetics, and attitudinal stance in #avotoast. *Internet Pragmatics*, *5*(2), 197–226. https://doi.org/10.1075/ip.00068.rap

3 Power

In March 2021, a TikTok video pitching the plot of a young adult (YA) fantasy novel went viral. Featuring a driving bass soundtrack and a sequence of dark fantasy/manga inspired images, it asked readers whether they would read a book about a "cursed island that appears once every hundred years to host a game that gives six rulers of a realm a chance to break their curses. Each realm's curse is deadly, and to break them, one of the six rulers must die" (Aster, 2021). Emblazoned in caption script across the images, the video promises that to break the curse and win the game the heroine will be required to "Lie, Cheat, Betray." The subsequent publication of Alex Aster's *Lightlark* (2022), the novel pitched in this viral TikTok, shows how successful engagement with the social reading culture of BookTok disrupted the power dynamic between gatekeepers that have traditionally mediated the acquisition of YA fiction. The traditional quality control processes supplied by the literary agent, the commissioning editor, or a competitive series of reviews acquisition by publishing executives were derailed. In enabling the viral marketing of a yet-unwritten manuscript, BookTok facilitated the retailing of internet celebrity (Abidin, 2018) rather than a good story (Johanson et al., 2022). An elaborate "art of the con" generated a book deal based on a strategy of pre-orders that ultimately disappointed readers when the expectations generated by the hype were not delivered.

Lightlark is an example of TikTok hype leading to the publication of a book ultimately rejected by many readers for failing to live up to its marketing. Our previous research with professionals in the Australian reading industry—primarily publishers, booksellers, authors, and agents—found the criterion of the "good story" to be crucial in shepherding a manuscript from potential acquisition to final publication (Johanson et al., 2022). The gatekeeping mechanisms of the reading industry have traditionally been trusted to ensure that new authors have the ability to craft a good read. The criticism of informed readers of *Lightlark* indicates that the novel as published fails the "good story" criteria. This example, which we return to later in this chapter, illustrates how the rise of bookish social media has altered the power dynamics in the reading industry. This chapter focuses on how the role of readers

DOI: 10.4324/9781003458616-4

as tastemakers sits in tension with marketing and promotional strategies that position authors as brands and seek to create affective parasocial relationships with a fan community of readers.

In the early 2000s, as new platforms lowered the threshold for the creation of user-generated content, cultural scholars celebrated a democratising of the public sphere that amplified the voices of "real" readers. As Driscoll (2019) writes in her analysis of the industry entanglements of literary blogs, the potential for the introduction of "new voices into public discussion was part of the excitement around" the introduction of blogs as a form. Fan-run blogs, as Jenkins (2006b) noted, became integral components of the creative industries, often collaborating "with corporate interests" but also providing "grassroots" feedback channels mediating the industry's lack of diversity (p. 151). As we discussed in the introduction to this book, starting a personal book blog can form part of a strategy to demonstrate bookish expertise and to establish and showcase relationships with professionals in the book industry, as well as demonstrate book love and a bookish identity. As we outline in the following, reader taste and author agency have the potential to destabilise comfortable promotional circuits by disrupting the ways traditional cultural intermediaries such as publishers, booksellers, and literary critics exercise influence in the reading industry.

Goodreads, the largest book-centred social media platform, has been the subject of much recent analysis of the "digitally-enabled literary community" (Murray, 2021, p. 972). In essence, Goodreads is a book-focused social cataloguing website that allows readers to curate personalised bookshelves and catalogue their books using a range of categories such as "currently reading," "TBR," favourite reads, and genre-based lists. The most studied feature of Goodreads are user book reviews, with user comments and star ratings analysed as public accounts of the reading experience (Driscoll & Rehberg Sedo, 2019) and a source of quantified reader reception (Murray, 2021). In addition to giving books a star rating, users can organise and participate in reader challenges, craft detailed reviews, and "demonstrate their standing as critics within the literary industry" (Murray, 2021, p. 978). Goodreads has had a significant impact on the distribution of power in the reading industry as a key platform for reader tastemaking and the performance of reader labour. It is also a vehicle for generating and receiving book recommendations with a gateway to retail opportunities, and a data-collection machine that influences consumer purchase and library acquisition decisions. As one of the first digital platforms to amplify reader voices (Driscoll, 2021), Goodreads cannot be excluded from any examination of reader labour and power relations. This chapter includes two case studies examining how reader influence in Goodreads is mobilised as part of the #ownvoices movement to critique stereotypical representation of diverse characters and promote marginalised writers.

In this chapter we explore a number of questions about the effects of bookish social media on the reading industry; in particular, its impact on the power dynamics between readers, authors, and traditional literary gatekeepers such as publishers, booksellers, and critics. We examine the strategies used to promote the author as a brand, the role of readers as tastemakers, and their parasocial affective relationship with writers and creators, as well as industry strategies to co-opt readers to aid their promotional campaigns. We also consider the implications of trope-based marketing of YA and romance fiction in response to trends on bookish social media. In doing so, we address the following research questions:

1. What is the impact of the book industry's ability to use social media to direct content to readers, bypassing traditional cultural intermediaries?
2. What role does reader taste and agency play in contributing to or disrupting circuits of recommendation and consumption?

The analysis in this chapter draws on interviews with book industry executives, social media creators, and focus groups with teen readers. A narrative analysis of journalistic and social media reviews of controversial titles suggested our case studies, while an ecological survey of book-related social media sites was used to identify the major platforms for reader tastemaking. We argue that digital social reading cultures offer increased agency and visibility to readers and book consumers within contemporary literary culture, and provide authors with alternative ways to publish and promote creative works.

Readers as tastemakers

A significant consequence flowing from the proliferation of bookish social media platforms is that publishers are able to "connect with readers directly and immediately" (Fuller & Rehberg Sedo, 2023), with larger firms deploying "complex algorithms" to capture data about reader tastes and market directly to them. According to one strand of analysis, algorithmic culture and direct publisher access to readers results in a narrowing of diversity and contracting reader horizons (Childress, 2017; Murray, 2021). As we have discussed elsewhere (Johanson et al., 2022), scholars have argued that recommendation algorithms "create statistical stereotypes" into which readers are straight-jacketed, suppressing readerly desire for new "reading territory" (Murray, 2021, p. 981). There is some debate about whether Goodreads ratings or TikTok endorsements are a result of publisher incentives such as funnelling advanced reader copies (ARCs) to influencers, paid "book tours" on blogs, bookish podcasts, and Instagram, rather than genuine reader demand or evaluation. Platforms themselves may exploit the connections between bookish fans and authors as is witnessed by the introduction of a TikTok Book Club (Navlakha, 2022) with direct retail purchase click-throughs, while publishers establish profiles that leverage the vernacular of sites to appeal to young readers. For example, as we discuss in Chapter 2, Penguin Teen, @penguin_teen on TikTok and @penguinteen on Instagram, is a particularly active publisher on bookish social media.

However, promoting titles cannot necessarily make readers like or recommend them (Miller, 2022). Publishers' direct conduits to readers also mean that readers become more important "agents within the reading industry," not only consuming bookish content on multiple channels, but as content creators they exert influence "within networked communities" (Fuller & Rehberg Sedo, 2023) with unpredictable consequences. This means they can act as unruly disrupters—not only forming part of a promotional circuit but also by writing back with ideological critique and challenge to existing industry practices. These disruptive practices include recommending books by authors from different identity groups and drawing attention to the politics of representation. We examine this further in two #ownvoices case studies that illustrate instances in which reader activism played a role in instigating awareness of the need for sensitivity editing and prompted awareness of the need for authentic voice in fiction.

#Ownvoices: reader taste and online advocacy

Existing research has comprehensively demonstrated the lack of diversity in English language publishing. Racial and ethnic homogeneity, for example, is apparent amongst authors represented (Bold, 2018, 2019; Booth & Narayan, 2018), company staff, content, target readership (Burns, 2012), and awards (Garrison, 2019; Johanson et al., 2022). However, online movements such as #ownvoices have been adopted by both bookish influencers and readers in bookish social media communities, and consequently have influenced publishers' commissioning decisions. Interviews with Australian publishers (Rutherford et al., 2022a) found a desire to include texts for more diverse readers hampered by publishers' own perceived lack of cultural understanding. YA #ownvoices novels were, however, recognised as generating genuine interest and engagement from audiences, prompting awareness in agents and publishers of reader sensitivity to authenticity of representation (Johanson et al., 2022, p. 8).

Goodreads is currently the primary platform for quantified reader reception of books while Twitter (now X) formerly gained a reputation as the site where controversies about representation, authenticity, and structural biases in the reading industry played out between authors, readers, and bookish influencers (Driscoll, 2021; Rosenfield, 2017). The #ownvoices movement launched on Twitter in 2015 when author and blogger Corrine Duyvis coined the hashtag to recommend works featuring the authentic voices of diverse authors (Duyvis, 2015). #Ownvoices is now a global movement providing "voice to the political opinions of readers that intervene in and call to account their local ecologies of publishing" (Booth & Narayan, 2020). In turn, debate and the spectre of reader backlash on social media channels has prompted change in the practices and promotional communications of the reading industry. #Ownvoices is cited as a criterion by reviewers in "editorial content" and by marketers "to highlight when an author is writing from their personal experiences in a marginalized group" (Vanderhage, 2019). In this context, bookish social media has become a vehicle for reader activism as well as the object of critique for its apparent unkindness to new authors. As we discuss in the following, Twitter and Goodreads campaigns have resulted in pile-on effects, virally magnifying ill-informed sentiment.

There are several recent cases of Twitter and Goodreads campaigns critiquing issues or representation in titles by newer YA authors, either delaying the publication of a text or occasioning a re-edit guided by professional sensitivity readers (see Lawrence, 2020). Driscoll notes the case of *The Continent*, a YA science fiction/romance story by Keira Drake (2018[2017]). Social media responses to the ARCs distributed by Harlequin Teen review-bombed the work, "objecting to its depiction of a white girl who brings peace to warring tribes and its use of stereotypes associated with Native American and Japanese cultures" (Driscoll, 2021). The book's publication was delayed by over a year as Drake undertook extensive revisions addressing these critiques (Shapiro, 2018). A similar experience delayed the publication of Amélie Wen Zhao's debut novel, *Blood Heir* (2020), following reader criticisms of the author's depiction of slavery as racially insensitive. The debate about the politics of representation opposed views critical of its supposed neglect of the sensitivities of African American readers to others arguing against the purported silencing of an Asian American author. Zhao, like Drake, elected to work with a sensitivity reader and found the experience educative (Alter, 2019; Hoggatt, 2019).

Authors and publishers frequently lament such critiques as a kind of censorship, limiting creativity and amplifying a herd response from those who may not even have read the book (Alter, 2019). Since Goodreads review ratings have commercial impact, such as influencing library orders, this platform remains a key site for reader influence. Ultimately, despite identity standpoint disagreements, these controversies highlight reader advocacy for a politics of representation that acknowledges the rights of readers from marginalised identity groups not to be subject to limited, stereotyped, or insensitive depictions.

#Ownvoices: risk-minimisation and industry power

Industry recognition of readers' appetite for authentic #ownvoices fiction has also influenced publisher promotional strategies. This case study discusses the strategies used by an Australian publisher to legitimise the publication of a first-person novel about a trans teenager written by an established, but cishet author. Craig Silvey's *Honeybee* (2020) was marketed as a significant

Australian cultural product with strong educative potential. It tells the story of Sam/Victoria as they struggle towards an adult identity as a trans woman in the face of family trauma and maternal rejection. The publisher, Allen and Unwin, argued that this coming-of-age narrative provided a vehicle for identification for trans and non-binary readers while also offering "empathic education for other young readers" (Rutherford et al., 2022b). This promotional strategy was designed to counteract charges of appropriation and ultimately prevailed despite many strong negative reviews on social media and some equivocal reviews in mainstream outlets accusing the author of stereotypical representation, trauma mining, and poor allyship.

Anticipating resistance to Silvey's choice of voice in *Honeybee*, the publisher orchestrated a series of mainstream press interviews to seed two central narratives; firstly, they detailed the writer's extensive research with the trans community—recruiting it discursively as an ally; secondly, they stressed the educative agenda of the book for both LGBTQI+ and heteronormative readers. In a *Sydney Morning Herald* article, aptly subbed with a title that anticipates reader backlash, Silvey's publisher, Jane Palfreyman, anticipated #ownvoices challenges to the appropriation of a trans voice, citing the "moving responses" of young transgender people to the novel:

> We feel we have done everything we can to be as respectful as possible and I stand by that. I think it is a beautiful book and I think Craig has a real gift for empathy and making a reader feel part of someone's life and feelings . . . that is the great power that writers have.
>
> (Kembrey, 2020)

Other pre-publication strategies included the distributing of ARCs to Goodreads reviewers and, despite the appeal to an educational motive on behalf of young readers, a careful distancing of the book from the YA label. This strategy responds to the vulnerability of YA titles to negative social media critique for insensitive representation of marginalised identities (see Irankunda, 2020). Despite having a teenaged protagonist and several other adolescent characters *Honeybee* was not marketed as YA fiction but as one of "four big Australian novels being released at the sweet end of the publishing year, when shoppers are beginning to contemplate which books to give as stocking stuffers for Christmas" (Hyde, 2020).

Australia is a small publishing market and therefore risk-minimising strategies are essential to justify the acquisition of potentially controversial titles. To a large extent, this strategy was successful, with Goodreads reviewers of *Honeybee* who rated the book at the highest 5-stars typically reiterating elements of the pre-publication industry narrative such as the intensive research with and outreach to the LGBTQI+ community and the novel's potential to lead cisgender readers to more stories featuring trans experience. Several thank the publisher for providing them an ARC (Rutherford et al., 2022b), indicating the success of a marketing strategy designed to build publicity for a "major new release" (Driscoll, 2021), as well as illustrating the promotional role of reviewers as part of the reading industry.

However, not all readers accepted the publisher's narrative about endorsement and positive reception from non-binary readers. Hyde's review also cites an #ownvoices author and educator on the structural biases within the reading industry that make such a response plausible: "[T]here is a very real possibility that this book will be well-received by many young trans readers . . . [but] it is taking up space that could be filled by work written by trans and gender diverse writers" (Hyde, 2020). Many Goodreads reviewers made similar points. A survey of 1-star ratings identified the following heads of critique: inauthenticity, or major deficiencies in representation of the everyday reality experienced by non-binary or gender-diverse persons; (2) appropriation; (3) consistent depiction of physical and psychological violence against a trans youth for entertainment purposes; and (4) writing that focuses on stereotyping characters or genre tropes that are marginal to the main arc of the story (Rutherford et al., 2022b). The bad faith of the reading industry is a common theme. Platforming a white cisgender male to speak for trans experience denies creative and representational justice and recognition. A review by a trans man in *The Guardian* succinctly makes the point that genuine allyship necessitates "knowing when and how to use your platform to lift others up" rather than attempting to capture their experiences; "sometimes, it just means knowing how to take a step back" (Gallagher, 2020).

The author as a brand

Authors also leverage social media and social reading practices to create an audience for their books. Authors use several of the strategies we identified in Chapter 1 to establish their literary credentials and create social and personal connections with readers. Similar to how bookish influencers create bookish social media content to establish their cultural and social capital as expert readers (Fuller & Rehberg Sedo, 2023), some authors engage with bookish social media to establish their personal brand as authentic storytellers. One example is Colleen Hoover's strategic self-promotion across all forms of digital bookish social media. Our case study of Hoover's marketing savvy examines how the viral success of one of her backlist titles during the COVID-19 pandemic resulted in the publication of a sequel and created a huge social media fandom. Our second case study is on a smaller scale. It documents the transition of an Australian writer, C. G. Drews, from prolific bookish social media creator to subscription-model self-publisher. This case study illustrates how an author-influencer can leverage their profile as a social media celebrity and their knowledge of new digital dissemination and promotional affordances to exploit the parasocial relationships generated by their "relational labour" (Baym, 2015). Our third case study illustrate how the development of a parasocial relationship based on a "perceived interconnectedness" (Abidin, 2018) is undermined if reader expectations are not met.

Colleen Hoover—Queen of #BookTok

Mainstream press articles about Hoover's career as an author commonly begin with a recitation of her recent dominance of bestseller lists. A narrative of unexpected, almost inexplicable success is contrasted with her small-town roots to emphasise the unlikeliness of her current status as the "Queen" of BookTok. Veltman's (2022) interview for National Public Radio is a representative example:

> The top-selling author in the country right now is a 42-year-old mom and former social worker who lives in the same small Texas town where she's spent practically her entire life. Colleen Hoover's romance-heavy reads are regular fixtures on bestseller lists. . . . Despite all of the success, Hoover tries her best to cling on to the trappings of ordinary life.

The success of Hoover—CoHo to her fans—is often attributed to grassroots reader activity on BookTok. For example, Gamerman and Wong observe that "with the help of fans who call themselves CoHorts," Hoover's books have outperformed more established authors to occupy "eight of the top 15 spots" on the New York Times bestseller list in 2022. These BookTokers "show off heavily annotated copies while swooning over their 'book boyfriends' . . . and sharing emotional time-lapses of themselves reading her novels" (Gamerman & Wong, 2022). This journalistic trope results in less attention being paid to Hoover's own strategic self-promotion using the affordances of multiple social media platforms.

As part of the struggler-to-success narrative, critics often note that Hoover's first novel, *Slammed* (2012), was self-published "because she wanted to share the story with her grandmother, who had just gotten a Kindle" (Merry, 2022). Self-publishing has always been an option for aspiring authors but when Amazon launched its Kindle e-reader in 2007, it also introduced Kindle Direct Publishing which significantly lowered the bar for the publication and promotion of e-books (Britannica, 2023) while at the same time ensuring a ready supply of content for its new e-reading platform. Previous self-publishing print-on-demand services had allowed authors to upload e-books in pdf format, whereas Amazon Direct "dramatically increased the number of self-published [e-books] available in a remarkably short time. Perhaps even more important, it introduced a new financial model into the self-publishing arena" (Bradley et al., 2011).

Both online retailers and traditional publishers were alert to the ways in which self-published work could provide market testing for new authors and genres. However, despite press interviews that reiterate Hoover's narrative about her non-commercial motivation for publishing alongside her naïve surprise at the exponential growth of the sales of *Slammed*, Hoover tactically used social media marketing to promote her book's visibility from the outset. As *Slate* magazine's Miller (2022) explains:

> Hoover has been a savvy self-promoter since 2012, when she distributed free copies of her first, self-published YA novel, *Slammed*, to influential book bloggers. She was big on BookTube (the YouTube book community) and big on 'Bookstagram' well before TikTok came along.

Kate, one of the social media creators we interviewed, confirmed this observation: "Colleen Hoover is extraordinarily popular on TikTok. She was very popular on BookTube, but it was maybe three or four years ago" (interview, 31 August 2022).

As we discuss in Chapter 1, the performance of enthusiasm is an important marker of the identity of bookish influencers as authentic book lovers. This enthusiasm prioritises passion and enjoyment as the hallmarks of genuine reader responses directed at a community of engaged readers bonded by their reading taste. TikTok's meme and music driven short-video formula exploits this "feels culture" (Stein, 2015). Hoover's novels are particularly suited to BookTok because "the platform favors big, grabby displays of emotion, as opposed to the tasteful lifestyle curation of Instagram" (Miller, 2022). They speak to readers who value emotional experience rather than craft. As we canvassed in Chapter 1, "crying on TikTok," as somewhat puzzled, mainstream press reporters have documented, has become an unexpected yet powerful means to promote books (Harris, 2021; Merry, 2022). Numerous BookToks created by Hoover's readers—"CoHorts"—show their fervent reaction to her books as they film themselves "sobbing, screaming, gasping in astonishment" (Miller, 2022). Examples of this include @kierralewis75's "This book got me crying, screaming, throwing up," (Lewis, 2022) and @eloisehamp's "I cried for an hour after reading this book" (Hampson, 2021).

One of the reasons for Hoover's popularity on bookish social media (and that of YA romance and genre fiction in general) is its appeal to those who may not formerly have considered themselves readers. Miller's clear-eyed yet sympathetic analysis of Hoover's prose makes clear that the "blandness of Hoover's characters," the "smooth, featureless quality of her prose," and the lack of atmospheric passages devoted to world-building facilitates easy identification and guarantees a quick read. Her books appeal to "non-readers" who seek the direct route to emotional experience without wasting time on extraneous plot development or wordy descriptions of place. Amanda, one of the social media creators we interviewed, echoes this view in her description of BookTok books as "books for people who don't actually like reading,"

> which is wonderful—is seriously so wonderful if people like reading and if people get into reading, that's something to be celebrated. But it's like the Colleen Hoovers of the world, and I've tried two Colleen Hoover books, and I just don't get it. Not only do I not get it, I really hated them. Really hated them. I find they tend to be that sort of romancy sort of section—which I do really like romance, but just not that cheap and cheesy for me."
> (interview, 14 October 2022)

Timing is another factor in Hoover's BookTok success. The effects of the COVID-19 pandemic and limits to mobility and sociality associated with lockdowns had a significant impact on the reading industry. Sales of print and e-books soared in 2020–21, especially titles popular on BookTok including *We Were Liars* (Lockhart, 2014), *They Both Die at the End* (Silvera, 2017), and, of course, Hoover's *It Ends with Us* (Kaplan, 2022). As we discussed in Chapter 1, one of the surprising features of this increase in book sales was the unexpected demand for backlist titles. Hoover's *It Ends with Us*, a significant beneficiary of this trend, was originally published in 2016. However, due to BookTokers' video endorsements in 2020 and 2021, it was propelled to the "second best-selling Adult Fiction book and sixth best-selling book overall in 2021" in the US market. For the book industry, TikTok's unpredictable virality proved a major disrupter of supply chains. As BookTokers captured themselves sobbing over their favourite reads, including *It Ends with Us*, this unexpected demand for backlist titles confounded the book industry.

C. G. Drews

The Boy Who Steals Houses (2019) (TBWSH) is a realist, issues-based Australian YA novel with an #ownvoices author. It features two siblings, both homeless and the former victims of family violence. Sam, the protagonist, "steals houses," breaking and occupying to provide shelter for Avery, his brother, and his evolving family. Sam keeps the keys of places he has visited as a kind of emotional anchor. The themes of identity and diversity, emotional upheaval, neurodiversity, and "found family" suggest a primary market in education, particularly school libraries anxious to support their students' identity pathways. As the New York Public Library blog explained, "family of choice" narratives, "where a group of characters find themselves united in a family-bond based on shared experiences, mutual understanding, and interpersonal connection," may have particular resonance for disenfranchised identity groups "such as those in the LGBTQ+ community" (Vélez, 2020). Alongside tags such as "Age from c. 12 years," "Romance and relationship stories," and "Children's/teen family and home stories," Drews's publisher, Hachette Australia, explicitly lists her debut title *A Thousand Perfect Notes*

(2018) as suitable for the UK's National Curriculum Key Stages 3, 4, and GCSE (Hachette, 2023).[1]

TBWSH might be classified as a prestige publication intended more to accrue reputation to a publisher through prizes and critical acclaim than to generate high-volume sales (Dane, 2020). Such titles may be set on curricula and achieve moderate longevity through library orders. TBWSH was awarded an Honour Book mention by the Children's Book Council of Australia in its older reader category in 2020; the CBCA prizes are awarded for literary merit rather than broad popular appeal (Children's Book Council of Australia, 2020). The publisher also nominated it for a Yoto Carnegie Medal in the same year, an award selected by children's librarians for an "outstanding book written in English for children and young people" (Yoto Carnegies, 2023). It has featured in themed lists such as #LoveOzYA's "Living with a Disability Reads" (LoveOzYA, 2022) where it is assigned the tag "autism."[2] Nevertheless the romance elements, the popularity of #ownvoices narratives amongst young adult readers, and the opportunity for reader emotion suggest the potential for a wider market for TBWSH (see Schoonens, forthcoming), particularly amongst readers open to engagement with a variety of fictional genres.

Drews's YA fiction has been moderately successful in a traditional publishing model. However her #ownvoices title, TBWSH, provides an example of the use of subscription and parasocial bookish membership models to finance creativity. As we discussed in Chapter 2, the author's prominence in online bookish social media communities provided a vehicle to reach this audience. Drews has an extensive social media presence across multiple platforms, including Tumblr, Instagram, Pinterest, and Twitter, where Drews is identified by the handle @paperfury (Schoonens, forthcoming). While Bookstagram is Drews's primary social media channel, it is only one of several bookish social media accounts. Drews is a Goodreads reviewer with a following of over 22,000, and a long-established book blogger with close to 20,000 subscribers, and has a more recent presence on TikTok (@cgdrews). Drews was able to leverage an existing follower and reader audience on Bookstagram and other bookish social media platforms to promote an experiment with alternative e-publishing models for the sequels to TBWSH.

Drews envisaged TBWSH as the first part of a series, apparently intending its sequel *The Kings of Nowhere* (2022a) (TKON) to be traditionally published. Drews's post on the blog (*paperfury.com*) on 3 April 2022, which was timed to coordinate with World Autism Day, was self-revelatory: "[T]his book that has existed alone in my head for 5 years" is now "out there." Outlining the author's journey to self-publishing on the Patreon platform, Drews (2022b) commented further:

> Publishing TKON came with a lot of heartache and battling feelings of failure. I worked my guts out trying to get this book to sell, but my experience with traditional publishing has always been a mess . . . but I just didn't want to let the TBWSH trilogy go. I'm so glad it gets to exist.

Patreon is a subscription-model crowdfunding platform that allows patrons to financially support creators (e.g., podcasters, musicians, authors, and more). It refers to itself as a membership platform (Regner, 2021); the term "membership" foregrounds the mutual relationships created between creators and those who appreciate their work. Unlike other crowdfunding platforms such as *Kickstarter* that mount single campaigns for a short period such as a couple of months, Patreon "facilitates the financial support of creators on a monthly basis" (Regner, 2021). For those who attract dedicated pledges, this can allow creators to devote at least a portion of their time to their creative work. Drews's Patreon page for TBWSH has 226 members at the time of writing and references a monthly income of AU $638 (*patreon.com/paperfury*) which places Drews in the higher band of creator income documented in Regner's study. Given the modest print runs for Australian YA new releases, this ongoing income stream may be a more substantial rate of return than might be expected from royalty payments on print book sales. Drews's Patreon subscribers receive electronic access to both sequels to TBWSH—TKON and *The House for Lost Things* (2023), as well as monthly Q&A sessions with the author.

Patreon members have the opportunity to withdraw their pledges at any time. The continued following thus indicates that these interactions and the affection for the world of TBWSH cements this parasocial relationship between Drews and the author's bookish fans. As we discussed in Chapter 1, bookish influencers leverage their performed identities to form social connections. Patreon "turns the one-off interaction between" author and readership into a "continuous relationship" (Regner, 2021, p. 133). This parasocial intimacy is similar to that experienced by Hoover's fans on BookTok and Bookstagram whose sense of community is such that they brand themselves as "CoHorts." These relationships based on book love and cohabitation of imaginative universes are dependent on the readers' sense of the authentic persona of the writer.

Alex Aster—Lightlark

Aster, BookToker and writer, represented herself on TikTok as an aspiring author who had struggled unsuccessfully with publisher rejections for a number of years. Her novel idea, which we previewed at the start of this chapter, was to convince potential readers to read her book, *Lightlark* (2022), based on its fantasy romance tropes alone. In subsequent videos, Aster promoted *Lightlark* as *A Court of Thorns and Roses* (ACOTAR) (Maas, 2015) meets *The Hunger Games* (Collins, 2008) featuring a more diverse cast (Messina, 2022; TwotheFuture, 2022). At the time of the initial pitch, Aster already had a substantial TikTok following. This public profile provided her with one of the key criteria for marketing her brand as an author. In addition, like many bookish influencers, she was skilled in video self-presentation with a heart-shaped face, long brown hair, and an engaging smile. As an attractive young woman of Latina extraction, rare characteristics among fantasy writers, her narrative generated high interest among would-be readers. According to Messina (2022):

> Within a week of her newfound internet fame, Aster's book went to auction, and she was offered a six-figure deal with Amulet Books. [She] continued to advertise her novel on TikTok leading up to its release on August 23. Videos filled with quotes from the novel and promises of classic young adult literary tropes such as rivals to lovers, a love triangle and the villain gets the girl, filled her TikTok profile.

Aster's success in obtaining a publishing contract without either a manuscript or ostensibly any track record as an author in the youth market flies in the face of the usual risk-averse acquisition practices of the industry. Even more surprisingly, the book was quickly optioned by a major studio without apparent evidence of a strong fan base of readers. This seems like a case of marketing based on pure internet celebrity (Abidin, 2018). While the studio faced little risk in optioning the book, since this did not in any way commit to production, the publisher's acquisition decision was an unusual gamble. At first glance, it appeared that the usual processes such as mediation by a literary agent, good sales of previous books, manuscript prizes, or—much more rarely—a compelling story pitched to and championed by an acquisitions editor via an open submission call were missing. As we discuss in the following, this narrative of inexperience and lack of credentials was inauthentic. Moreover, commissioning via premise and TikTok trope marketing led to a serious "breach of contract" with readers when the expected novelty and content were not delivered.

Aster's initial TikTok campaign building buzz around the novel and hyping its contents was highly successful. After initial videos promoting *Lightlark* as a combination of early romance fantasy hybrids, her subsequent TikToks either marketed the promised tropes, character interactions, and teasers for scenes the book promised to contain, or celebrated the author's newfound celebrity. The latter included videos from the publishing process, Aster's wide-eyed self-deprecation about her interview on ABC's morning news program *Good Morning America*, and videos showing her with "other large YA authors, like Chloe Gong, Adam Silvera, and Marie Lu, who appeared to be her friends" (ExtensionOne, 2022). Silvera and Gong, alongside other BookTok influencers, were among the first to post 5-star reviews for *Lightlark* on Goodreads with extremely truncated reviews reminiscent of cover jacket quotes. Pre-orders flowed in, and the double impact of BookTok influencer endorsement and the promise of a movie by "the producers of Twilight" seemed to assure quality. As ExtensionOne's Reddit explained: surely a book "picked up immediately by a publisher after hearing about it, generating so much positive buzz by booktok, reviewed by multiple prominent authors" had to be good? While many teen readers employ multiple verification strategies such as checking with other readers or consulting a number of online reviews before committing to purchase or borrow a book, others are social media populists who feel that if a book "blows up" on their feeds, "then I'm like well if everyone's reading it, I've got to try it. It must be good" (Rutherford & Reddan, 2024).

This early promise was quickly challenged once ARC reviews began to appear on Goodreads. These reviews were not good. In a matter of weeks *Lightlark*'s Goodreads star rating had fallen from 5 to around 2 (at the date of writing it is sitting at 3.72). The novel was pilloried as poorly structured with juvenile prose and insufficient worldbuilding:

> Aster's prose is slightly juvenile, even for YA, and repetitive, with strange phrases that should have been amputated by even a slightly proficient editor. Some small examples include:
>
> "It was a shining, cliffy thing" (referring to an island)
> "It was just a yolky thing" (referring to the sun)
> "she glared at him meanly" (as opposed to sweetly)
>
> (ExtensionOne, 2022)

However, the major critique of the content centred on breach of readerly expectations, namely that Aster had failed to deliver the book she had promised to write on TikTok. As the previously cited Redditor wryly suggested, many readers of fantasy romance are willing to trade hackneyed characters or dialogue and a "mediocre plot" for steamy scenes with "swoonworthy bad boys" (ExtensionOne, 2022). With respect to *Lightlark*, readers felt duped for other reasons. The novel Aster promised was not delivered as major scenes or sections of dialogue that featured in her videos were either changed beyond recognition or completely missing. More damningly, the diversity of representation hinted at also failed to materialise. Aster's TikToks had suggested that *Lightlark* would disrupt the convention that placed marginalised or diverse characters into secondary roles in genre fiction. When the novel was published, its major characters were all described as pale, with the one person of colour—also gay—depicted in a flatter and more tokenistic fashion (Bean, 2022).

Goodreads, as discussed previously, is an important hub in the infrastructure of the reading industry as a site of reader agency and reception. Many highly-engaged teen readers use Goodreads as an important source of reviews when judging whether to read a book that has been recommended to them either face to face or via their feeds (Rutherford & Reddan, 2024). The crux of the "Lightlark controversy" is that concerted "review bombing" lowered the initial pre-publication rating from 5/5 stars to below 2 stars in under a month. The first review to come up on Goodreads (at the date of writing) when you filter by 1-star is by "Bean" (Bean, 2022). It provides a good summary of reader criticism of the book and is worth analysing in some detail because it makes a clear case about how the novel breached reader expectations by failing to deliver the content that had been so relentlessly promoted:

> I picked up this book because of tiktok [sic] . . . Calling it pastiche would be kind. Each scene felt very reminiscent of something out of another YA book. Many, many YA books. So much of this book is borrowed from ACOTAR that any differentiation from the plot of ACOTAR felt like a subversion of story even if it made perfect sense within Lightlark's narrative. Also, I can proudly say that any comparison to the Hunger Games is unwarranted. *It's a terrible comparison that sets up false expectations.* More accurately, it's ACOTAR meets The Selection [Kiera Cass, 2013].
> (Bean, 2022; emphasis added)

Bean finds the dialogue "atrocious," the male leads ripped from the whole sheet of Sarah J. Maas's ACOTAR series. They argue that the "convoluted" worldbuilding without sufficient geopolitical detail or internal logic renders the stakes of the competitions motivated by the lands' curses fatally undeveloped, while the characterisation is based on flat telling rather than any nuanced internal focalisation. Bean says they know where the characters are "mentally" only because "the author would tell us. It's a common vice in YA." The writing reeks of "blatant explanations of Isla's struggle" mixed with "faux feminist ideology" that is clearly inspired by the worst excesses of "Sarah J. Maas' writing . . . Which kind of sucks, because [Maas's] prose isn't good either" (Bean, 2022).

Bean's review also makes a nuanced argument about the role of reader taste and agency influencing the success of trope marketing. They acknowledge that some readers do enjoy reading "100 different versions of the same book," that readers find comfort and excitement in books that suffer from flaws. Weigel, writing in the *Cleveland Review of Books* makes a similar point. Despite immediately identifying *Lightlark* as another "one of those YA" genre cutouts, a "story that's roughly five percent plot and ninety-five percent random jumbles of Mary Sue-led, instant-attraction-romance nonsense" (2022),[3] she is also seduced by the appeal of a "stupid, fun," if poorly written, YA read presented in an aesthetically appealing "vanity design," for example, each page having "thorn detailing on the edges." In this context, a discerning literary reader of well-crafted fantasy narrativises the pleasure promised by *Lightlark* while simultaneously deploring its exploitation of its readers and reading industry complicity in promoting sales over readers' rights to "good" stories. Readers read, this suggests, because of book love and denying the promised content fractures their contract with the writer. In a similar vein, Weigel argues that *Lightlark* is a "by the numbers" YA title, an "unoriginal, box-checking, phoned-in knockoff of a classic YA fantasy story."

Her critique reiterates the argument that readers have a right to expect a good story, as opposed to a "safe, market-tested consumable . . . a product first, book second" (2022).

Interestingly in light of our previous discussion of #ownvoices authors and the bookish social relationships between writers and readers, Aster suffered the heaviest backlash in reviews due to a perceived lack of authenticity in her representation of her identity on social media. In a nutshell, despite being a previously published middle-grade author with a literary agent and a wealthy family able to support her, Aster's TikToks presented a rags-to-riches narrative, depicting herself as a struggling POC writer having achieved wild success after decades of rejection. Her campaign, which was in fact carefully orchestrated by her media professional sister, sold this trope with a "set of carefully crafted phrases about how her many years of discouragement had ended in a movie deal with the producers of Twilight" (Weigel, 2022). The review bombing and the more critical readerly response to *Lightlark* are evidence of the corrective provided by reader agency. While it is difficult to gauge effects on actual sales (TwotheFuture, 2022), and the second volume in the series, *Nightbane* (Aster, 2023), was indeed published, many teen readers do decide between titles based on Goodreads and other review ratings (Rutherford & Reddan, 2024; Johanson et al., 2022). The pitfalls of Aster's personality marketing are, firstly, the inevitable exposure of the author's inauthenticity, which is a key facet of the parasocial relationship between authors and readers. More importantly, however, trope marketing or as one critic described it the "trope-ification of YA fantasy" threatens both story and genre diversity.

Tropes as aids to discovery and promotion

The focus on tropes on BookTok has influenced how readers talk about and seek to discover books. According to De Leon (2022), "tropes have become an internet shorthand to help people find their next read" on BookTok. Particularly in the romance genre, these are tags that typically describe aspects of the relationship arc, such as "enemies to lovers," "love triangles," though they often function to capture other aspects of characterisation or plot devices such as "morally grey characters," or "fake dating" as famously used in the first of the *Bridgerton* series of novels (De Leon, 2022). While not confined to TikTok, trope-based hashtags function as search terms and in tagging, curating, and list-making tools on platforms such as Goodreads, Instagram, and the fanfiction site, Archive of Our Own (AO3). However, TikTok's short video format makes the strategy particularly useful for BookTokers. As one content creator reported, you "have mere seconds to capture the attention of a viewer and condense the plot of a book. Tropes make the task easier" (Biino, 2023).

Focus groups conducted with both highly engaged and less regular teen readers, including readers who use BookTok to search for book recommendations, indicate that tropes are frequently used to identify potential reads (Rutherford & Reddan, 2024). Academic and romance author Roach explained the utility of tropes to ensure the "pleasure of familiarity which is part of what makes for an intimate, easy type of reading experience" (cited in De Leon, 2022). It is also an efficient strategy to find books suited to a reader's taste. Roach also astutely identified what is lost by such narrow searches:

> 'If you only ever look for your "second chance" romance tropes, for example, you're going to miss out on a lot of delightful storytelling that you might have been drawn to or found otherwise,' Roach said. 'It can be narrowing and limiting, but it can be efficient.'
>
> (De Leon, 2022)

There are multiple potential consequences arising from the use of tropes as a marketing strategy. Firstly, the tendency for publishers to include such tags in the book's metadata as well as on TikTok may influence book recommendations on the platform and potentially skew national bestseller lists. According to metrics from NDP BookScan and the *New York Times*, sales numbers for BookTok books almost doubled in 2021 and increased again in 2022 (De Leon, 2022). Secondly, authors may be pressured by other sectors of the reading industry to include tropes in their work to achieve greater sales or increase their chances of going viral on book social media. For some authors, such as Aster, this impetus led to a work that was highly derivative with a flawed narrative structure.

Some established authors described the pressure to market their books using tropes or to include elements of these while retaining their own voice and producing a well-crafted plot. Chloe Gong, one of *Lightlark*'s early endorsers, discussed the self-promotion of her stories that do not comfortably fit the mould of "Booktok Books": "[Y]ou tend to talk about the romance more, and the drama subplot more, and I think it's because that's what holds attention" (Biino, 2023). One historical novelist reported taking into account the keywords driving reader searches to maximise sales, crafting a book that was "still in my own voice, in my own plot, but that was able to fit into the enemies to lovers category" (Biino, 2023).

There is a caveat to this negative tendency. As the Aster identity controversy indicates, readers are not comfortable with the bad faith of authors who manipulate their texts to cash in on viral trends. In this context, readers engaged in bookish social media platforms including BookTok and Goodreads have expressed rejection of books in which character and plot are sacrificed to overuse of tropes—the "ninety-five percent random jumbles of Mary Sue-led, instant-attraction-romance nonsense" scathingly described by Weigel (2022). Plot and character are unfailingly the criteria readers cite as what keeps them reading a book after they have picked it up (vivafalastinleen,

2022). Tastemaking readers also use the criteria of the good story in their evaluations of genre fiction. As May, one of the engaged adolescent readers from our focus groups, commented:

> So lots of books are very over-rated . . . I feel like on BookTok it's just easily digested books . . . they're pretty trophy [trope-y], general stereotype . . . engaging enough for me to read through quickly but I wouldn't say they were like amazing. Only a few are [amazing].
>
> (May, year 10 student)

Conclusion

This chapter has examined how grassroots feedback channels and affective relationships with creators work to mediate the reading industry's lack of diversity, often destabilising commercial promotional circuits. While book influencers and reader-reviewers can be implicated in marketing campaigns that compromise impartiality, readers as tastemakers who campaign from gender, identity, and generational standpoints have successfully intervened in attempts to co-opt reader labour for purely marketing purposes. We have also canvassed the ways in which authors and bookish influencers perform relational labour that creates parasocial bonds between creators and those who enjoy their work. This in turn has provided pathways to alternative publication and circulation models that are based on reader rather than publisher indices of value. Finally, we have detailed the affordances and pitfalls of trope-based marketing on social media. This trend may narrow diversity of genre and narrative styles and limit the range of texts available to certain readers. However, importantly, it also addresses the tastes of a class of "non-literary" readers who value emotional experience in reading over the "good story."

Notes

1 GCSE in the United Kingdom stands for the General Certificate of Secondary Education. Australia does not offer separate evaluation and accreditation at this point in secondary schooling. Key stages 3 and 4 conform to years 7–9 in Australia when the students are 11–14 years of age.
2 #LoveOzYA, or the Australian Young Adult Reading Alliance, describes itself as a "national organisation promoting Australian youth literature, supporting diverse representation and 'own voices' in Australian YA" (https://loveozya.com.au/about/).
3 A "Mary-Sue" is a stereotypical or idealised female character, possessed of exceptional qualities and abilities, extreme attractiveness, and virtue, that is lacking in any major character flaws. The term had its origin in *Star Trek* fanfiction (Oxford English Dictionary, 2023).

Reference list

Abidin, C. (2018). *Internet celebrity: Understanding fame online*. Emerald Publishing Ltd. https://doi.org/10.1108/9781787560765

Alter, A. (2019). She pulled her debut book when critics found it racist. Now she plans to publish. *The New York Times*. www.nytimes.com/2019/04/29/books/amelie-wen-zhao-blood-heir.html#after-story-ad-2

Aster, A. [@alex.aster]. (2021). Would you buy a book about? It's called Lightlark [video]. *Tiktok*. www.tiktok.com/@alex.aster/video/6939242279056035077

Aster, A. (2022). *Lightlark*. Abrams Books.

Aster, A. (2023). *Nightbane*. Abrams Books.

Baym, N. K. (2015). Connect with your audience! The relational labor of connection. *The Communication Review*, *18*(1), 14–22.

Bean. (2022). Lightlark: Bean's goodreads review. [Post]. *Goodreads*. www.goodreads.com/review/show/4883581653

Biino, M. (2023, June 2). TikTok loves book tropes like 'enemies to lovers' and 'right person wrong time,' and authors are feeling pressure to use them to try and go viral. *Business Insider*. www.businessinsider.com/booktok-tropes-authors-pressure-tiktok-books-romance-2023-5

Bold, M. R. (2018). The eight percent problem: Authors of colour in the British young adult market (2006–2016). *Publishing Research Quarterly*, *34*(3), 385–406. https://doi.org/10.1007/s12109-018-9600-5

Bold, M. R. (2019). *Inclusive young adult fiction: Authors of colour in the United Kingdom*. Pan Macmillan.

Booth, E., & Narayan, B. (2018). Towards diversity in young adult fiction: Australian YA authors' publishing experiences and its implications for YA librarians and readers' advisory services. *Journal of the Australian Library and Information Association*, *67*(3), 195–211. https://doi.org/10.1080/24750158.2018.1497289

Booth, E., & Narayan, B. (2020). "The expectations that we be educators": The views of Australian authors of young adult fiction on their ownvoices novels as windows for learning about marginalized experiences. *Journal of Research on Libraries and Young Adults*, *11*(1). https://www.yalsa.ala.org/jrlya/wp-content/uploads/2020/02/Expectations_Booth_Narayan_FINAL.pdf

Bradley, J., Fulton, B., Helm, M., & Pittner, K. A. (2011). Non-traditional book publishing. *First Monday*, *16*(8). https://doi.org/10.5210/fm.v16i8.3353

Britannica, T. E. o. E. (2023). Kindle. In *Encyclopedia Britannica*. www.britannica.com/technology/Kindle

Burns, A. (2012). Multicultural body image in children's and young adult publishing. *The International Journal of Diversity in Organizations, Communities, and Nations: Annual Review*, *11*(3), 103–110. https://doi.org/10.18848/1447-9532/CGP/v11i03/39019

Cass, K. (2013). *The selection*. Harper Teen.

Children's Book Council of Australia. (2020). *The boy who steals houses*. CBCA. https://cbca.org.au/resources/the-boy-who-steals-houses

Childress, C. (2017). Decision-making, market logic and the rating mindset: Negotiating BookScan in the field of US trade publishing. *European Journal of Cultural Studies*, *15*(5), 604–620. https://doi.org/10.1177/1367549412445757

Collins, S. (2008). *The hunger games*. Scholastic.

Dane, A. (2020). *Gender and prestige in literature: Contemporary Australian book culture*. Palgrave Macmillan. https://doi.org/10.1007/978-3-030-49142-0

De Leon, R. (2022). TikTok figured out an easy way to recommend books. The results were dubious. *Slate*. https://slate.com/culture/2022/12/booktok-trope-sales-romance-fantasy-genre.html

Drake, K. (2018 [2017]). *The continent*. Harlequin Teen.

Drews, C. J. (2018). *A thousand perfect notes*. Hachette Australia.

Drews, C. J. (2019). *The boy who steals houses*. Hachette Australia.

Drews, C. J. (2022a). *The kings of nowhere*. Patreon.

Drews, C. J. (2022b, April 3). *The kings of nowhere is officially out now! Paperfury*. https://paperfury.com/the-kings-of-nowhere-is-officially-out-now/

Drews, C. J. (2023). *The house for lost things*. Patreon.

Driscoll, B. (2019). Book blogs as tastemakers. *Participations: Journal of Audience and Reception Studies, 16*(1), 280–305. www.participations.org/16-01-14-driscoll.pdf

Driscoll, B. (2021, June 15). How Goodreads is changing book culture. *Kill Your Darlings*. www.killyourdarlings.com.au/article/how-goodreads-is-changing-book-culture/

Driscoll, B., & Rehberg Sedo, D. (2019). Faraway, so close: Seeing the intimacy in Goodreads reviews. *Qualitative Inquiry, 25*(3), 248–259. https://doi.org/10.1177/1077800418801375

Duyvis, C. (2015). *#OwnVoices*. www.corinneduyvis.net/ownvoices/

ExtensionOne [ExtensionOne]. (2022). [Booktok] How TikTok hype got a YA novel published, then immediately cancelled the author for being an industry plant [Post]. *Reddit*. www.reddit.com/r/HobbyDrama/comments/xfdgts/booktok_how_tiktok_hype_got_a_ya_novel_published/?rdt=45437

Fuller, D., & Rehberg Sedo, D. (2023). *Reading bestsellers: Recommendation culture and the multimodal reader*. Cambridge University Press. https://www.cambridge.org/core/elements/reading-bestsellers/8C6D9254C5B8C6DD87714DE3A98CEA77

Gallagher, A. (2020, October 16). Why should trans people trust non trans authors to lead the conversation about our identities? *The Guardian*. www.theguardian.com/books/2020/oct/16/why-should-trans-people-trust-non-trans-authors-to-lead-the-conversation-about-our-identities

Gamerman, E., & Wong, A. (2022, October 18). How Colleen Hoover conquered the bestseller list. *The Wall Street Journal*. www.wsj.com/articles/colleen-hoover-new-book-11666105107

Garrison, K. L. (2019). What's going on Down Under? Part 2: Portrayals of culture in award-winning Australian young adult literature. *Journal of Research on Libraries and Young Adults, 10*(2), 1–34. www.yalsa.ala.org/jrlya/2019/07/whats-going-on-down-under-part-2-portrayals-of-culture-in-award-winning-australian-young-adult-literature/

Hachette. (2023). *A thousand perfect notes: C.G. Drews*. Hachette Australia. www.hachette.com.au/cg-drews/a-thousand-perfect-notes

Hampson, E. [@eloisehams] (2021). *I cried for an hour after reading this book*. [Video] *Tiktok*. www.tiktok.com/@eloisehamp/video/6942754389962525958

Harris, E. A. (2021, March 21). How crying on Tiktok sells books. *The New York Times*. www.nytimes.com/2021/03/20/books/booktok-tiktok-video.htm

Hoggatt, A. (2019, January 31). An author canceled her own YA novel over accusations of racism. But is it really anti-black? *Slate.* https://slate.com/culture/2019/01/blood-heir-ya-book-twitter-controversy.html

Hoover, C. (2012). *Slammed.* Atria Books.

Hoover, C. (2016). *It ends with us.* Atria Books.

Hyde, J. (2020, September 30). Craig Silvey on writing from a trans perspective: 'A novelist is required to listen, to learn'. *The Guardian.* www.theguardian.com/books/2020/sep/30/craig-silvey-on-writing-from-a-trans-perspective-a-novelist-is-required-to-listen-to-learn

Irankunda, L. (2020, September 18). Identity policing in YA: Becky Albertalli's heartfelt coming out essay opens up an important conversation. *The Mary Sue.* www.themarysue.com/identity-policing-in-ya-becky-albertallis-heartfelt-coming-out-essay-opens-up-an-important-conversation/

Jenkins, H. (2006b). *Fans, bloggers, and gamers: Exploring participatory culture.* New York University Press.

Johanson, K., Rutherford, L., & Reddan, B. (2022). Beyond the "good story" and sales history: Where is the reader in the publishing process? *Cultural Trends, 32*(2), 91–106. https://doi.org/10.1080/09548963.2022.2045864

Kaplan, A. (2022). How TikTok helped fuel the best-selling year for print books. *Forbes.* https://www.forbes.com/sites/annakaplan/2022/01/28/how-tiktok-helped-fuel-the-best-selling-year-for-print-books/

Kembrey, M. (2020, September 25). Craig Silvey's new novel is bound to face intense scrutiny. He's OK with that. *The Sydney Morning Herald.* www.smh.com.au/culture/books/craig-silvey-s-new-novel-is-bound-to-face-intense-scrutiny-he-s-ok-with-that-20200925-p55z4h.html

Lawrence, E. E. (2020). Is sensitivity reading a form of censorship? *Journal of Information Ethics, 29*(1), 30–44.

Lewis, K. [@kierralewis] (2022). *This book got me. crying, screaming, throwing up!"*. [Video] *Tiktok.* www.tiktok.com/@kierralewis75/video/7118853654970420522

Lockhart, E. (2014). *We were liars.* Delacorte Press.

LoveOzYA. (2022). Living with a disability: #LoveOzYAreads. *LoveOzYA: Read local.* https://loveozya.com.au/loveozya-living-with-a-disability-reads/

Maas, S. J. (2015). *A court of thorns and roses.* Bloomsbury.

Merry, S. (2022, January 22). On TikTok, crying is encouraged. Colleen Hoover's books get the job done. *The Washington Post.* www.washingtonpost.com/books/2022/01/20/colleen-hoover-tiktok/

Messina, J. (2022, September 15). Lightlark: The very first clickbait novel. *Daily Trojan.* https://dailytrojan.com/2022/09/15/lightlark-the-very-first-clickbait-novel/

Miller, L. (2022, August 7). The unlikely author who's absolutely dominating the bestseller list. *Slate.* https://slate.com/culture/2022/08/colleen-hoover-books-it-ends-with-us-verity.html

Murray, S. (2021). Secret agents: Algorithmic culture, Goodreads and datafication of the contemporary book world. *European Journal of Cultural Studies, 24*(4), 970–989. https://doi.org/10.1177/1367549419886026

Navlakha, M. (2022). #BookTok rejoice: TikTok launches official Book Club. *Mashable.* https://mashable.com/article/tiktok-book-club-launch

Oxford English Dictionary (2023). Mary Sue. In *Oxford English Dictionary*. Retrieved December 18, 2023, from www.oed.com/dictionary/mary-sue_n?tl=true

Regner, T. (2021). Crowdfunding a monthly income: An analysis of the membership platform Patreon. *Journal of Cultural Economics, 45*(1), 133–142. https://doi.org/10.1007/s10824-020-09381

Rosenfield, K. (2017). The toxic drama of YA Twitter. *Vulture: New Yorker Magazine*. www.vulture.com/2017/08/the-toxic-drama-of-ya-twitter.html

Rutherford, L., Johanson, K., & Reddan, B. (2022a). *Cultural pathways to teen reading: Publishing industry challenges*. Teen Reading in the Digital Era—Deakin University. https://teenreading.net/publications-reports/

Rutherford, L., Johanson, K., & Reddan, B. (2022b). #Ownvoices, disruptive platforms, and reader reception in young adult publishing. *Publishing Research Quarterly, 38*, 573–585. https://doi.org/10.1007/s12109-022-09901-5

Rutherford, L., & Reddan, B. (2024). Finding a good read? Strategies Australian teenagers use to negotiate book recommendations. In C. E. Loh (Ed.), *The reading lives of teens*. Routledge.

Schoonens, A. (forthcoming). *The digital media ecologies of young adult fiction: Teen readers and participatory culture*. Queensland University of Technology.

Shapiro, L. (2018, February 19). Can you revise a book to make it more woke? *Vulture*. www.vulture.com/2018/02/keira-drake-the-continent.html

Silvera, A. (2017). *They both die at the end*. Harper Teen.

Stein, L. (2015). *Millennial fandom: Television audiences in the transmedia age*. University of Iowa Press.

TwotheFuture. (2022). *The 'fyre festival' of Tiktok: Lightlark*. Retrieved November 8, from www.youtube.com/watch?v=5fuZX-J8JMc

Vanderhage, G. (2019). What is #ownvoices? *Brodart Books and Library Services*. www.brodartbooks.com/newsletter/posts-in-2019/what-is-ownvoices

Vélez, E. (2020, November 22). Found family: Literature that celebrates choice. *NYPL Blog*. www.nypl.org/blog/2020/12/09/found-family-literature-celebrates-families-choice

Veltman, C. (2022, October 24). Author Colleen Hoover went from tending cows to writing bestsellers. *National Public Radio*. www.npr.org/2022/10/24/1129735256/colleen-hoover-bestselling-author-releases-new-novel-it-starts-with-us

vivafalastinleen [@leen]. (2022). Little spiel on #booktropes inspired by @maebbi's recent vid!! [Video]. *Tiktok*. www.tiktok.com/@vivafalastinleen/video/7124040348392852779

Weigel, A. (2022, July 11). The Trope-ification of YA Fantasy and its marketing: On Alex Aster's "Lightlark". *Cleveland Review of Books*. www.clereviewofbooks.com/writing/alex-aster-lightlark-ya-fantasy

Yoto Carnegies. (2023). *About the awards*. https://yotocarnegies.co.uk/about-the-awards/

Zhao, A. (2019). *Blood heir*. Delacorte Press.

Conclusion
The place of books in digital spaces

> [S]ocial media has changed a lot . . . it's actually a lot less social than it used to be
> —Victoria (interview, 7 June 2023)

Social reading practices will continue to evolve alongside digital technologies. While the proliferation of bookish social media content indicates that readers will continue to engage with books and reading in digital spaces, change, as Victoria observes, is a constant feature of the digital media landscape. Victoria, one of the bookish content creators interviewed as part of the DAGR project, made this observation about a decrease in the sociality of social media in response to a question about how much time she spends creating content for and managing her bookish social media accounts and whether this has changed over time. Victoria's reflection on a decrease in the amount of social chat on social media is based on her decade of experience as a bookish content creator. In place of the banter she exchanged with like-minded creatives on Twitter in the early 2010s, Victoria experiences contemporary bookish social media as a more curated digital space in which promotion is more prominent than social connection. Like many bookish influencers, Victoria makes strategic choices about how to use social media to support her "core business" activities as an author. While engagement with bookish social media remains an important tool in developing parasocial relationships with communities of readers, Victoria devotes less labour to it now because it is "not as much of a focus as it used to be."

To some extent, Victoria's experience of change in the culture of the bookish social media communities she participates in reflects the impact of life stage and platform affordances on the way users engage with social media. It is no coincidence that the amount of time Victoria spends creating bookish social media content has decreased as she has honed her skills as a content creator and transitioned from an emerging fiction writer to an established author with a public profile. Platform affordances, as we discussed in Chapter 1, also play an important role in shaping the culture of bookish social media communities.

DOI: 10.4324/9781003458616-5

Conclusion

In Victoria's example, it is the shift from short text-based content on Twitter to the visual culture of Instagram's beautiful bookish aesthetic that contributes to her perception of an increase in curation and promotion. However, this example also points to change in the broader social media environment as we discussed in the introduction and Chapter 1. Digital media scholarship, including work by Abidin (2015, 2018, 2020) and Burgess and Green (2018), map shifts in the way influencers develop parasocial relationships through the performance of relational (Baym, 2018) and affective (Papacharissi, 2015) labour. These key concepts have informed our analysis of bookish social media, and each of the three chapters in this book have examined a different aspect of the relational and affective labour performed by bookish influencers and readers, and the parasocial relationships produced by this labour.

Our goal in writing this book was to explore how bookish content on digital social media platforms is influencing readers and reading practices by providing a digital space for readers to engage with books and each other. We began this task in the introduction by providing an overview of key influences on the social life of books and reading in contemporary Western literary culture. The introduction identified social media platforms as key sites for the performance of bookishness, performances which demonstrate the cultural significance of books in the post-digital era as well as the co-existence of digital and analogue book technologies. It also situated the development of bookish social media in the context of celebrity book club culture and convergence in book and digital culture. It argued that the entanglement of celebrity, commerce, and culture in celebrity book clubs and the affordances of bookishness in the post-digital era have had significant impacts on the social reading cultures developed in bookish social media communities.

Chapter 1 examined how the affordances of YouTube, Instagram, and TikTok shape how readers engage in social reading practices on each platform. It illustrated how bookish influencers use multiple strategies to establish their bookish identity and create social and personal connections with bookish audiences. It also analysed similarities and differences in the types of social reading cultures developed on BookTube, Bookstagram, and BookTok, and the ways platform affordances shape the performance of relational and affective labour. In doing so, we do not suggest that there is something fundamentally different about how readers read in the post-digital age but that the affordances of the social media platforms have created new environments in which social reading practices are flourishing. This analysis identified differences in the way book culture is constituted on each platform, differences we interpret as indicators of the development of distinct social reading cultures on BookTube, Bookstagram, and BookTok. BookTube offers the impression of conversation with a knowledgeable bookish friend. Bookstagram evokes the sensory pleasures of reading through curation of beautiful displays of books and bookish objects. BookTok appeals to readers who want to get swept up in emotion. This snapshot of the contemporary landscape of bookish social

Conclusion 81

media is intended encourage discussion about the role of social reading cultures in contemporary literary culture.

Chapter 2 analysed digital practices prominent in bookish communities on YouTube, Instagram, and TikTok. It examined the types of practices used to enact bookish identities and encourage parasocial relationships between influencers and readers on BookTube, Bookstagram, and BookTok. Two case studies focused on socio-material practices on TikTok and Instagram as examples of how the creative labour of influencers performs the aesthetic of bookishness in social reading cultures. Two case studies on the performance of passion for books and reading on YouTube emphasise the parasocial implications of the creation of relatable bookish content, including diversification in users' reading habits and the development of innovative pathways to book authorship and reading. This chapter argued that practices which celebrate the materiality of books and reading are an integral part of social reading cultures, and that digital social media platforms offer opportunities to reimagine book and reading culture.

Chapter 3 explored the effects of bookish social media on the reading industry with a focus on the power dynamics of reader labour on Goodreads and the role of parasocial bonds in providing alternative pathways to publication and circulation of creative works. Two case studies of #ownvoices reader activism reflected on the role of readers as tastemakers and the ability of grassroots feedback channels to mediate a lack of diversity in the reading industry. Three case studies analysed the strategies used by publishers and authors to position authors as brands, and involve readers in their promotional campaigns, with emphasis on how such strategies produce, or alternatively undermine, the development of affective parasocial relationships between authors and readers. It also considered the implications of trope-based marketing for reader discovery and author creativity. This chapter argued that the creation of new opportunities for readers to engage in social reading practices on bookish social media has elevated the agency and visibility of readers and book consumers within contemporary literary culture and provided authors with alternative pathways to publication and promotion of creative works.

As digital technologies continue to evolve, the ways in which readers express their bookish identities, talk about books and reading, and connect with other readers will also change. As Fuller and Rehberg Sedo (2023) observe, "if a platform can be used for booktalk, then readers will find it and figure out a way to share their reading experiences on it" (p. 33). This means that digital social reading cultures will continue to respond to changes in the digital media environment, as will performances of bookishness. For example, as we discussed in Chapter 2, new creator and fan practices related to narrative and story-worlds will emerge, and it will be important to continue to interrogate the connections and disconnections between new forms of bookish content and the reading industry. Developing a passion for books and bookish content may not necessarily emerge from exposure to printed books or traditionally published materials. As the Stacy Hinojosa case study illustrates, young readers may develop their passion for story through a games-based story world, or through being introduced to traditional books via a gaming platform.

The enmeshment of reading and digital culture (Murray, 2018) explored in this book raises a number of questions about the future dimensions of digital social reading cultures. Will future readers develop a passion for books via Metaverse worlds in which they are able to experience stories in virtual space, as they currently can via a Meta Quest gaming headset? Which bookish practices in metaverse spaces resemble current practices, and what kinds of new ones will emerge? How will generative artificial intelligence (Generative AI) change how creators make content for social media platforms? Will new story forms, authorship, and fan practices emerge from the possibilities of Generative AI? These are significant questions because currently popular digital platforms like YouTube, Instagram, and TikTok will eventually give way to new popular platforms, or at the very least will have to compete with new platforms. Many bookish practices will have continuities with contemporary social reading cultures, but some will be innovative and unexpected because they reinterpret and reinscribe the cultural significance of books and reading for new audiences.

Reference list

Abidin, C. (2015). Communicative ♥ intimacies: Influencers and perceived interconnectedness. *Ada: A Journal of Gender, New Media, and Technology*, *8*. https://doi.org/10.7264/N3MW2FFG

Abidin, C. (2018). *Internet celebrity: Understanding fame online*. Emerald Publishing.

Abidin, C. (2020). Mapping internet celebrity on TikTok: Exploring attention economies and visibility labours. *Cultural Science Journal*, *12*(1), 77–103. https://doi.org/10.5334/CSCI.140

Baym, N. K. (2018). *Playing to the crowd: Musicians, audiences, and the intimate work of connection*. New York University Press.

Burgess, J., & Green, J. (2018). *YouTube—Online video and participatory culture*, 2nd ed. Polity Press.

Fuller, D., & Rehberg Sedo, D. (2023). *Reading bestsellers: Recommendation culture and the multimodal reader*. Cambridge University Press. www.cambridge.org/core/elements/reading-bestsellers/8C6D9254C5B8C6DD87714DE3A98CEA77

Murray, S. (2018). *The digital literary sphere: Reading, writing, and selling books in the internet era*. JHU Press.

Papacharissi, Z. (2015). *Affective publics: Sentiment, technology and politics*. Oxford University Press.

Bibliography

Abidin, C. (2015). Communicative ♥ intimacies: Influencers and perceived interconnectedness. *Ada: A Journal of Gender, New Media, and Technology, 8*. https://doi.org/10.7264/N3MW2FFG

Abidin, C. (2016). Visibility labour: Engaging with Influencers' fashion brands and #OOTD advertorial campaigns on Instagram. *Media International Australia, 161*(1), 86–100. https://doi.org/10.1177/1329878X16665177

Abidin, C. (2018). *Internet celebrity: Understanding fame online*. Emerald Publishing.

Abidin, C. (2020). Mapping internet celebrity on TikTok: Exploring attention economies and visibility labours. *Cultural Science Journal, 12*(1), 77–103. http://doi.org/10.5334/csci.140

Albrecht, K. (2017). *Positioning BookTube in the publishing world: An examination of online book reviewing through the field theory* [Master's thesis, Leiden University]. Leiden University student repository. https://hdl.handle.net/1887/52201

Alter, A. (2019). She pulled her debut book when critics found it racist. Now she plans to publish. *The New York Times*. www.nytimes.com/2019/04/29/books/amelie-wen-zhao-blood-heir.html#after-story-ad-2

Amazon (n.d.). *Wild rescuers* (4 book series). Retrieved December 14, 2023, from www.amazon.com/Wild-Rescuers-4-book-series/dp/B07KY4VGMF

Anderson, M., Faverio, M., & Gottfried, J. (2023). *Teens, social media and Technology 2023*. Pew Research Centre. www.pewresearch.org/internet/wp-content/uploads/sites/9/2023/12/PI_2023.12.11-Teens-Social-Media-Tech_FINAL.pdf

Arriagada, A., & Ibáñez, F. (2020). "You need at least one picture daily, if not, you're dead": Content creators and platform evolution in the social media ecology. *Social Media + Society, 6*(3), 1–12. https://doi.org/10.1177/2056305120944624

Aster, A. [@alex.aster]. (2021). It's called Lightlark #booktok #bookstan #bookclub #yabooks #books. [Video]. *Tiktok*. www.tiktok.com/@alex.aster/video/6939242279056035077

Aster, A. (2022). *Lightlark*. Abrams Books.

Aster, A. (2023). *Nightbane*. Abrams Books.

Barad, K. (2003). Posthumanist performativity: Toward an understanding of how matter comes to matter. *Signs: Journal of Women in Culture and Society, 28*(3), 801–831. https://doi.org/10.1086/345321

Barnett, B. (2023, August 6). "I can't stress how much BookTok sells": Teen literary influencers swaying publishers. *The Guardian*. www.theguardian.com/books/2023/aug/06/i-cant-stress-how-much-booktok-sells-teen-literary-influencers-swaying-publishers

Baym, N. K. (2015). Connect with your audience! The relational labor of connection. *The Communication Review*, *18*(1), 14–22. https://doi.org/10.1080/10714421.2015.996401

Baym, N. K. (2018). *Playing to the crowd: Musicians, audiences, and the intimate work of connection*. New York University Press. https://doi.org/10.2307/j.ctv12pnpcg

Bean. (2022). Lightlark: Bean's goodreads review. [Post]. *Goodreads*. www.goodreads.com/review/show/4883581653

Biino, M. (2023, June 2). TikTok loves book tropes like 'enemies to lovers' and 'right person wrong time,' and authors are feeling pressure to use them to try and go viral. *Business Insider*. www.businessinsider.com/booktok-tropes-authors-pressure-tiktok-books-romance-2023-5

Birke, D. (2021). Social reading? On the rise of a "bookish" reading culture online. *Poetics Today*, *42*(2), 149–172. https://doi.org/10.1215/03335372-8883178

Birke, D. (2023). "Doing" literary reading online: The case of Booktube. In A. Ensslin, J. Round, & B. Thomas (Eds.), *The Routledge companion to literary media* (pp. 468–478). Taylor & Francis Group.

Birke, D., & Fehrle, J. (2018). #booklove: How reading culture is adapted on the internet. *Komparatistik Online*, 60–86. www.komparatistik-online.de/index.php/komparatistik_online/article/view/191

Bold, M. R. (2018). The eight percent problem: Authors of colour in the British young adult market (2006–2016). *Publishing Research Quarterly*, *34*(3), 385–406. https://doi.org/10.1007/s12109-018-9600-5

Bold, M. R. (2019). *Inclusive young adult fiction: Authors of colour in the United Kingdom*. Pan Macmillan.

Booth, E., & Narayan, B. (2018). Towards diversity in young adult fiction: Australian YA authors' publishing experiences and its implications for YA librarians and readers' advisory services. *Journal of the Australian Library and Information Association*, *67*(3), 195–211. https://doi.org/10.1080/24750158.2018.1497349

Booth, E., & Narayan, B. (2020). "The expectations that we be educators": The views of Australian authors of young adult fiction on their ownvoices novels as windows for learning about marginalized experiences. *Journal of Research on Libraries and Young Adults*, *11*(1). https://www.yalsa.ala.org/jrlya/wp-content/uploads/2020/02/Expectations_Booth_Narayan_FINAL.pdf

boyd, d. (2014). *It's complicated: The social lives of networked teens*. Yale University Press.

Bradley, J., Fulton, B., Helm, M., & Pittner, K. A. (2011). Non-traditional book publishing. *First Monday*, *16*(8). https://doi.org/10.5210/fm.v16i8.3353

Branagh-Miscampbell, M., & Marsden, S. (2019). "Eating, sleeping, breathing, reading": The Zoella book club and the young woman reader in the 21st century. *Participations: Journal of Audience and Reception Studies*, *16*(1), 412–440. www.participations.org/16-01-20-branagh-miscampbell.pdf

Brandt, D. (1998). Sponsors of Literacy. *College Composition and Communication*, *49*(2), 165–185. https://doi.org/10.2307/358929

Britannica, T. E. o. E. (2023). Kindle. In *Encyclopedia Britannica*. www.britannica.com/technology/Kindle

Burgess, J., & Green, J. (2018). *YouTube—Online video and participatory culture* (2nd ed.). Polity Press.

Burkell, J., Regan, P. M., & Steeves, V. (2022). Privacy, consent, and confidentiality in social media research. In A. Quan-Haase & L. Sloan (Eds.), *The SAGE handbook of social media research methods* (pp. 715–725). SAGE Publications. https://doi.org/10.4135/9781529782943.n50

Burns, A. (2012). Multicultural body image in children's and young adult publishing. *The International Journal of Diversity in Organizations, Communities, and Nations: Annual Review*, *11*(3), 103–110. https://doi.org/10.18848/1447-9532/CGP/v11i03/39019

Burwell, C., & Miller, T. (2016). Let's play: Exploring literacy practices in an emerging videogame paratext. *E-Learning and Digital Media*, *13*(3–4), 109–125.

Cass, K. (2013). *The selection*. Harper Teen.

Chaudhary, A. [@aymansbooks]. (2021, March 7). @penguin_teen CHECK OUT #HouseofHollow #PenguinTeenPartner #PenguinTEen #bookrec #booktok. [Video]. *TikTok*. www.tiktok.com/@aymansbooks/video/6936600453106978054

Children's Book Council of Australia. (2020). *The boy who steals houses*. CBCA. https://cbca.org.au/resources/the-boy-who-steals-houses

Childress, C. (2017). Decision-making, market logic and the rating mindset: Negotiating BookScan in the field of US trade publishing. *European Journal of Cultural Studies*, *15*(5), 604–620. https://doi.org/10.1177/1367549412445757

Chittal, N. (2018, December 19). Instagram is helping save the indie bookstore. *Vox*. www.vox.com/the-goods/2018/12/19/18146500/independent-bookstores-instagram-social-media-growth

Collins, J. (2010). *Bring on the books for everybody: How literary culture became popular culture*. Duke University Press.

Collins, S. (2008). *The hunger games*. Scholastic.

Cunningham, S., & Craig, D. (2017). Being 'really real' on YouTube: Authenticity, community and brand culture in social media entertainment. *Media International Australia*, *164*(1), 71–81. https://doi.org/10.1177/1329878X17709098

Dane, A. (2020). *Gender and prestige in literature: Contemporary Australian book culture*. Palgrave Macmillan. https://doi.org/10.1007/978-3-030-49142-0

Dane, A. (2021). Goodreads reviewers and affective fan labour. In A. Dane & M. Weber (Eds.), *Post-digital book cultures* (pp. 57–79). Monash University Publishing.

Dane, A., & Weber, M. (Eds.). (2021). *Post-digital book cultures*. Monash University Publishing.

Davis, M. (2017). Who are the new gatekeepers? Literary mediation and post-digital publishing. In A. Mannion, M. Weber, & K. Day (Eds.), *Publishing means business: Australian perspectives* (pp. 125–146). Monash University Publishing.

De Leon, R. (2022). TikTok figured out an easy way to recommend books. The results were dubious. *Slate*. https://slate.com/culture/2022/12/booktok-trope-sales-romance-fantasy-genre.html

DeRosa, V. P. (2017, June 21). I'm a teenager and I don't like young adult novels. Here's why. *Huffpost*. www.huffpost.com/entry/what-ya-gets-wrong-about-teenagers-from-a-teen_b_594a8e4de4b062254f3a5a94

Dexter, R. (2022, 12 March). The reading renaissance: could the #BookTok bump save publishing? *The Sydney Morning Herald*. www.smh.com.au/national/subbed-but-holding-for-next-sunday-the-reading-renaissance-could-the-booktok-bump-save-publishing-20220302-p5a109.html

Dezuanni, M. (2020). *Peer pedagogies: Learning with Minecraft let's play videos*. The MIT Press.

Dezuanni, M., Reddan, B., Rutherford, L., & Schoonens, A. (2022). Selfies and shelfies on #bookstagram and #booktok—social media and the mediation of Australian teen reading. *Learning, Media and Technology*, *47*(3), 355–372. https://doi.org/10.1080/17439884.2022.2068575

Dowling, D. (2019). *Immersive longform storytelling: Media, technology, audience*. Routledge.

Drake, K. (2018). *The continent* (reprint). Harlequin Teen. (Original work published 2017).

Drews, C. G. (2018). *A thousand perfect notes*. Hachette Australia.

Drews, C. G. (2019). *The boy who steals houses*. Orchard Books.

Drews, C. G. [@Paperfury]. (2022). *The kings of nowhere*. Patreon.

Drews, C. G. [@Paperfury]. (2023). *The house for lost things*. Patreon.

Driscoll, B. (2008). How Oprah's book club reinvented the woman reader. *Popular narrative media*, *1*(2), 139–150. https://doi.org/10.3828/pnm.1.2.3

Driscoll, B. (2014). *The new literary middlebrow: Tastemakers and reading in the twenty-first century*. Palgrave Macmillan.

Driscoll, B. (2016). Readers of popular fiction and emotion online. In K. Gelder (Ed.), *New directions in popular fiction: Genre, distribution, reproduction* (pp. 425–449). Palgrave Macmillan. https://doi.org/10.1057/978-1-137-52346-4_21

Driscoll, B. (2019). Book blogs as tastemakers. *Participations: Journal of Audience and Reception Studies*, *16*(1), 280–305. www.participations.org/16-01-14-driscoll.pdf

Driscoll, B. (2021, June 15). How Goodreads is changing book culture. *Kill Your Darlings*. www.killyourdarlings.com.au/article/how-goodreads-is-changing-book-culture/

du Gay, P., & Pryke, M. (2002). Cultural economy: An introduction. In P. du Gay & M. Pryke (Eds.), *Cultural economy: Cultural analysis and commercial life* (pp. 1–19). Sage.

Duyvis, C. (2015). *#OwnVoices*. www.corinneduyvis.net/ownvoices/

Ellis, D. (2021a, January 6). *The most popular books on TikTok*. BookRiot. https://bookriot.com/most-popular-books-on-tiktok/

Ellis, D. (2021b, May 26). *The past, present, and future of BookTube, according to BookTubers*. BookRiot. https://bookriot.com/booktube-according-to-booktubers/

Ellis, D. (2021c, July 19). *"It's gay and it slaps": TikTok's favorite LGBTQ books*. BookRiot https://bookriot.com/its-gay-and-it-slaps-books/

ExtensionOne [ExtensionOne]. (2022). *[Booktok] How TikTok hype got a YA novel published, then immediately cancelled the author for being an industry plant*. [Post]. Reddit. www.reddit.com/r/HobbyDrama/comments/xfdgts/booktok_how_tiktok_hype_got_a_ya_novel_published/?rdt=45437

Evans, A., & Riley, S. (2023). *Digital feeling*. Palgrave Macmillan.

Feeney, C. [@LittleBookOwl]. (2020). read with me 🐚 calming nature sounds & music. [Video]. YouTube. www.youtube.com/watch?v=GW3vlvFEC3U

Fisher, T. (2019). *The wives*. Graydon House.

Foasberg, N. M. (2012). Online reading communities: From book clubs to book blogs. *The Journal of Social Media in Society*, *1*(1), 30–53. https://thejsms.org/index.php/JSMS/article/view/3/4

Fuller, D., & Rehberg Sedo, D. (2013). *Reading beyond the book: The social practices of contemporary literary culture*. Routledge. https://doi.org/10.4324/9780203067741

Fuller, D., & Rehberg Sedo, D. (2023). *Reading bestsellers: Recommendation culture and the multimodal reader*. Cambridge University Press. www.cambridge.org/core/elements/reading-bestsellers/8C6D9254C5B8C6DD87714DE3A98CEA77

Gallagher, A. (2020, October 16). Why should trans people trust non trans authors to lead the conversation about our identities? *The Guardian*. www.theguardian.com/books/2020/oct/16/why-should-trans-people-trust-non-trans-authors-to-lead-the-conversation-about-our-identities

Gamerman, E., & Wong, A. (2022, October 18). How Colleen Hoover conquered the bestseller list. *The Wall Street Journal*. www.wsj.com/articles/colleen-hoover-new-book-11666105107

Garrison, K. L. (2019). What's going on down under? Part 2: Portrayals of culture in award-winning Australian young adult literature. *Journal of Research on Libraries and Young Adults*, *10*(2), 1–34. www.yalsa.ala.org/jrlya/2019/07/whats-going-on-down-under-part-2-portrayals-of-culture-in-award-winning-australian-young-adult-literature/

Ghaffary, S. & Heath, A. (2019, July 27). Why Instagram broke its square [Audio podcast episode]. In *Land of the giants*. Vox. www.vox.com/recode/23274761/facebook-instagram-land-the-giants-mark-zuckerberg-kevin-systrom-ashley-yuki

Gleasure, R., O'Reilly, P., & Cahalane, M. (2017). Inclusive technologies, selective traditions: A socio-material case study of crowdfunded book publishing. *Journal of Information Technology*, *32*, 326–343. https://doi.org/10.1057/s41265-017-0041-y

Gomez, J. (2005). Thinking outside the blog: Navigating the literary blogosphere. *Publishing Research Quarterly*, *21*(3), 3–11.

Grady, C. (2019, September 13). How Reese Witherspoon became the new high priestess of book clubs. *Vox.* www.vox.com/the-highlight/2019/9/13/20802579/reese-witherspoon-reeses-book-club-oprah

Grant Bruce, M. (1935). *Wings above Billabong.* Ward, Lock.

Green, J. (2012). *The fault in our stars.* Penguin.

Green, J. (2017). *Turtles all the way down.* Penguin.

Grochowski, S. (2020, March 5). PenguinTeen finds success on TikTok with viral video. *Publishers Weekly.* www.publishersweekly.com/pw/by-topic/childrens/childrens-industry-news/article/82611-penguinteen-finds-success-on-tiktok-with-viral-video.html

Hachette. (2023). *A thousand perfect notes: C.G. Drews.* Hachette Australia. www.hachette.com.au/cg-drews/a-thousand-perfect-notes

Hall, R. M. (2003). The "Oprahfication" of literacy: Reading "Oprah's Book Club". *College English, 65*(6), 646–667.

Hampson, E. [@eloisehams] (2021). I cried for an hour after reading this book. [Video]. *Tiktok.* www.tiktok.com/@eloisehamp/video/6942754389962525958

Harris, E. A. (2021, March 20). How crying on TikTok sells books. *New York Times.* www.nytimes.com/2021/03/20/books/booktok-tiktok-video.html

Hartley, J. (2001). *Reading groups.* Oxford University Press.

Haupt, A. (2019, August 6). The Bookstagrammers and BookTubers changing the way we read. *The Washington Post.* www.washingtonpost.com/entertainment/books/the-bookstagrammers-and-booktubers-changing-the-way-we-read/2019/08/06/60b76d6a-afb6-11e9-8e77-03b30bc29f64_story.html

Hawley, S. (2022). Doing sociomaterial studies: The circuit of agency. *Learning Media and Technology, 47*(4), 413–426. https://doi.org/10.1080/17439884.2021.1986064

@hayaisreading. (2022). #QOTD can you guess which movie this is? [Photograph]. *Instagram.* www.instagram.com/p/CbdGBrZsjRK/

Hinojosa, S. [@stacyplays]. (2014a, March 9–2021, May 16). Dogcraft. [Video series]. *YouTube.* www.youtube.com/playlist?list=PLc5xWgIisSO3CYeJFSzAX5fali9K_Uxwy

Hinojosa, S. [@stacyplays]. (2014b, October 15). The first book! Bookcraft (Ep. 3). [Video]. *YouTube.* www.youtube.com/watch?v=tFidJQ2ilug

Hinojosa, S. [@stacyplays]. (2015, August 29). Island of the blue dolphins: Bookcraft (CH.61). [Video]. *YouTube.* www.youtube.com/watch?v=PFihZUWV2_c

Hinojosa, S. [StacyPlays]. (2018–). *Wild rescuers series.* HarperCollins.

Hinojosa, S. [@stacyplays]. (2020, January 1). Journey to the centre of the Earth: Bookcraft. [Video]. *YouTube.* www.youtube.com/watch?v=OGiU2H4NUhA

Hinojosa, S. [@stacyplays]. (2021a, May 16). Page's rainbow bridge: Dogcraft (Ep. 342). [Video]. *YouTube.* www.youtube.com/watch?v=jcARqP8rW1Y

Hinojosa, S. [StacyPlays]. (2021b). *Sentinels in the deep ocean.* HarperCollins.

Hinojosa, S. [@stacyplays]. (2023, September 24). Welcome to Camp Friendly! #Minecraftyourstory. [Video]. *YouTube*. www.youtube.com/watch?v=0bKhili6t9Y

Hinojosa, S. [StacyPlays]. (2024–). *Rescue tails*. HarperCollins.

Hoggatt, A. (2019, January 31). An author canceled her own YA novel over accusations of racism. But is it really anti-black? *Slate*. https://slate.com/culture/2019/01/blood-heir-ya-book-twitter-controversy.html

Hoover, C. (2012). *Slammed*. Atria Books.

Hoover, C. (2016). *It ends with us*. Atria Books.

Hoover, C. (2022). *It starts with us*. Atria Books.

Horton, K. (2021). *BookTube and the publishing industry: A study of the commercial relationship between YouTube content creators and publicists* [Unpublished master's thesis]. Curtin University.

Hosein, S. [@booksaremysociallife]. (2021). Is the book community American-centric? [Video]. *YouTube*. www.youtube.com/watch?v=mHNckAuNYvk

Hunt, E. (2022, December 12). Legally bookish: Reese Witherspoon and the boom in celebrity book clubs. *The Guardian*. www.theguardian.com/books/2022/dec/12/legally-bookish-reese-witherspoon-and-the-boom-in-celebrity-book-clubs

Hyde, J. (2020, September 30). Craig Silvey on writing from a trans perspective: 'A novelist is required to listen, to learn'. *The Guardian*. www.theguardian.com/books/2020/sep/30/craig-silvey-on-writing-from-a-trans-perspective-a-novelist-is-required-to-listen-to-learn

Irankunda, L. (2020, September 18). Identity policing in YA: Becky Albertalli's heartfelt coming out essay opens up an important conversation. *The Mary Sue*. www.themarysue.com/identity-policing-in-ya-becky-albertallis-heartfelt-coming-out-essay-opens-up-an-important-conversation/

Ito, M., Baumer, S., Bittanti, M., boyd, d., Cody, R., Herr-Stephenson, B., Tripp, L. (2009). *Hanging out, messing around, and geeking out: Kids living and learning with new media*. The MIT Press.

Jacobs, C. [@caitsbooks]. (2020, July 21). Go check out @penguin_teen to learn more about this book! #houseofHollow #booktok #coverreveal #fyp #books. [Video]. *TikTok*. www.tiktok.com/@caitsbooks/video/6851593415046581510

Jacobs, C. (2021, March 7). This just made me realize that i need more floral stuff @penguin_teen #HouseofHollow (sic). [Video]. *TikTok*. www.tiktok.com/@caitsbooks/video/6936572647119572230

Jacobs, C. [@caitsbooks]. (n.d.). [TikTok Profile]. *TikTok*. Retrieved December 21, 2023, from www.tiktok.com/@caitsbooks

Jacobson, J., & Gorea, I. (2022). Ethics of using social media data in research: Users' views. In A. Quan-Haase & L. Sloan (Eds.), *The SAGE handbook of social media research methods* (pp. 703–714). SAGE Publications. https://doi.org/10.4135/9781529782943.n49

Jenkins, H. (2006a). *Convergence culture: Where old and new media collide*. New York University Press.

Jenkins, H. (2006b). *Fans, bloggers, and gamers: Exploring participatory culture*. New York University Press.

Jerasa, S., & Boffone, T. (2021). BookTok 101: TikTok, digital literacies, and out-of-school reading practices. *Journal of adolescent & adult literacy*, *65*(3), 219–226. https://doi.org/10.1002/JAAL.1199

Johanson, K., Rutherford, L., & Reddan, B. (2022). Beyond the "good story" and sales history: Where is the reader in the publishing process? *Cultural Trends*, *32*(2), 91–106. https://doi.org/10.1080/09548963.2022.2045864

Kelly, H. (2018, October 29). Here's an annoying new Instagram trend: Throwing yourself on a pile of open books. *Vulture*. www.vulture.com/2018/10/the-terrible-instagram-trend-of-piles-of-open-books.html

Kembrey, M. (2020, September 25). Craig Silvey's new novel is bound to face intense scrutiny. He's OK with that. *The Sydney Morning Herald*. www.smh.com.au/culture/books/craig-silvey-s-new-novel-is-bound-to-face-intense-scrutiny-he-s-ok-with-that-20200925-p55z4h.html

Kemp, S. (2023, October 19). *Digital 2023 October global statshot report*. DataReportal, Meltwater & We Are Social. https://datareportal.com/reports/digital-2023-october-global-statshot

Kennedy, M. (2020). 'If the rise of the TikTok dance and e-girl aesthetic has taught us anything, it's that teenage girls rule the internet right now': TikTok celebrity, girls and the Coronavirus crisis. *European Journal of Cultural Studies*, *23*(6), 1069–1076. https://doi.org/10.1177/1367549420945341

Khamis, S., Ang, L., & Welling, R. (2017). Self-branding, 'micro-celebrity' and the rise of social media influencers. *Celebrity Studies*, *8*(2), 191–208. https://doi.org/10.1080/19392397.2016.1218292

Kiernan, A. (2011). The growth of reading groups as a feminine leisure pursuit: Cultural democracy or dumbing down? In D. Rehberg Sedo (Ed.), *Reading communities from salons to cyberspace* (pp. 123–139). Palgrave Macmillan.

Kitchener, C. (2017, December 1). Why so many adults love young-adult literature. *The Atlantic*. www.theatlantic.com/entertainment/archive/2017/12/why-so-many-adults-are-love-young-adult-literature/547334/

Kokko, S. (2023). *Encouraging Reading on Social Media. Exploring Finnish Bookstagram Community* [Master's thesis, University of Gothenburg]. GUPEA. https://gupea.ub.gu.se/handle/2077/79256

Lawrence, E. E. (2020). Is sensitivity reading a form of censorship? *Journal of Information Ethics*, *29*(1), 30–44.

Leaver, T., Highfield, T., & Abidin, C. (2020). *Instagram: Visual social media cultures*. Polity Press.

Lee, M. & Lee, E. [@alifeofliterature]. (2021). convincing you to read books based off their aesthetics: we were liars by e. lockhart. [Video]. *TikTok*. www.tiktok.com/@alifeofliterature/video/6929091762107469062

Lewis, K. [@kierralewis] (2022). This book got me. crying, screaming, throwing up! [Video]. *Tiktok*. www.tiktok.com/@kierralewis75/video/7118853654970420522

Lockhart, E. (2014). *We were liars*. Delacorte Press.

Long, E. (2003). *Book clubs: Women and the uses of reading in everyday life*. University of Chicago Press.

Maas, S. J. (2015). *A court of thorns and roses*. Bloomsbury.

MacTavish, K. (2021). The emerging power of the Bookstagrammer: Reading #bookstagram as a post-digital site of book culture. In A. Dane, & M. Weber (Eds.), *Post-digital book cultures* (pp. 80–112). Monash University Publishing.

Marsden, S. (2018). "I didn't know you could read": Questioning the legitimacy of Kim Kardashian-West's status as a cultural and literary intermediary. *LOGOS: The Journal of the World Book Community*, *29*(2/3), 64–79. https://doi.org/10.1163/18784712-02902008

Martens, M., Balling, G., & Higgason, K. A. (2022). #BookTokMadeMeReadIt: Young adult reading communities across an international, sociotechnical landscape. *Information and Learning Sciences*, *123*(11/12), 705–722. https://doi.org/10.1108/ILS-07-2022-0086

Marwick, A. E. (2015). Instafame: Luxury selfies in the attention economy. *Public Culture*, *27*(75), 137–160. https://doi.org/10.1215/08992363-2798379

Marwick, A. E. (2017). Microcelebrity, self-branding, and the internet. *The Blackwell Encyclopedia of Sociology*, 1–3. https://doi.org/10.1002/9781405165518.WBEOS1000

McCall, T. (2022, November 18). BookTok's Racial Bias. *New York Magazine: The Cut*. www.thecut.com/2022/11/booktok-racial-bias-tiktok-algorithm.html

Merga, M. K. (2021). How can Booktok on TikTok inform readers' advisory services for young people? *Library & Information Science Research*, *43*(2), 1–10. https://doi.org/10.1016/J.LISR.2021.101091

Merry, S. (2022, January 22). On TikTok, crying is encouraged. Colleen Hoover's books get the job done. *The Washington Post*. www.washingtonpost.com/books/2022/01/20/colleen-hoover-tiktok/

Messina, J. (2022, September 15). Lightlark: The very first clickbait novel. *Daily Trojan*. https://dailytrojan.com/2022/09/15/lightlark-the-very-first-clickbait-novel/

Miller, L. (2022, August 7). The unlikely author who's absolutely dominating the bestseller list. *Slate*. https://slate.com/culture/2022/08/colleen-hoover-books-it-ends-with-us-verity.html

Miller, M. (2011). *The song of Achilles*. Ecco Press.

Milner, R. M. (2009). Working for the text: Fan labor and the new organization. *International Journal of Cultural Studies*, *12*(5), 491–508. https://doi.org/10.1177/1367877909337861

Mosseri, A. [@mosseri]. (2021, July 1). We're no longer just a square photo-sharing app. [Video]. *Instagram*. www.instagram.com/tv/CQwNfFBJr5A/

Murray, S. (2018). *The digital literary sphere: Reading, writing, and selling books in the internet era*. JHU Press.

Murray, S. (2020). *Introduction to contemporary print culture: Books as media*. Taylor & Francis.

Murray, S. (2021). Secret agents: Algorithmic culture, Goodreads and datafication of the contemporary book world. *European Journal of Cultural Studies*, *24*(4), 970–989. https://doi.org/10.1177/1367549419886026

Navlakha, M. (2022). #BookTok rejoice: TikTok launches official Book Club. *Mashable*. https://mashable.com/article/tiktok-book-club-launch

Nelson, M. (2006). The blog phenomenon and the book publishing industry. *Publishing Research Quarterly*, *22*(2), 3–26. https://doi.org/10.1007/S12109-006-0012-6

Nielsen BookData. (2022). *Understanding the UK young adult consumer 2022*. Nielsen Book Services. www.book2look.com/book/GdFrVqffD2

Notley, T. (2009). Young people, online networks, and social inclusion. *Journal of Computer-Mediated Communication, 14*(4), 1208–1227. https://doi.org/10.1111/j.1083-6101.2009.01487x

O'Connell, M. (2022, September 30). Reese Witherspoon and Lauren Neustadter are doing just fine without the boys' club. *The Hollywood Reporter.* www.hollywoodreporter.com/tv/tv-features/reese-witherspoon-lauren-neustadter-hello-sunshine-sale-big-little-lies-1235228211/

O'Meara, V. (2019). Weapons of the chic: Instagram influencer engagement pods as practices of resistance to Instagram platform labor. *Social Media + Society, 5*(4),1–11. https://doi.org/10.1177/2056305119879671

Oakley, T. (2015). *Binge.* Simon & Schuster.

Ofcom. (2023). *Children's Media Lives 2023: A report for Ofcom.* www.ofcom.org.uk/__data/assets/pdf_file/0025/255850/childrens-media-lives-2023-summary-report.pdf

Oxford English Dictionary (2023). Mary Sue. In *Oxford English Dictionary.* Retrieved December 18, 2023, from www.oed.com/dictionary/mary-sue_n?tl=true

Papacharissi, Z. (2015). *Affective publics: Sentiment, technology and politics.* Oxford University Press.

Penguin Teen [@penguin_teen]. (2020a, July 21). House of Hollow COVER REVEAL + recreation challenge! #booktok #books #houseofhollow #krystalsutherland. [Video]. *TikTok.* www.tiktok.com/@penguin_teen/video/6851594184055409926

Penguin Teen [@penguin_teen]. (2020b, February 9). Pls don't let this flop it's a miracle i still have a job #foryou #fyp #fy #dominos #books #officelife #viral (sic). [Video]. *TikTok.* www.tiktok.com/@penguin_teen/video/6791228381066169606?q=%22book%20domino%22%20%23penguinteen%202020&t=1702724064281

Penguin Teen [@penguin_teen]. (2021, May 13). The #unsolved case of the Somerton man + some epic Vivi cosplay from #HouseofHollow author @krystal_sutherland! #booktok. [Video]. *TikTok.* www.tiktok.com/@penguin_teen/video/6961514637280038149

Perkins, K. (2017). The boundaries of BookTube. *Serials Librarian, 73*(3–4), 352–356. https://doi.org/10.1080/0361526X.2017.1364317

Pham, C. [@withcindy]. (2018a, August 16). Unboxing soap gate. [Video]. *YouTube.* www.youtube.com/watch?v=iaj-UO5X2RQ&

Pham, C. [@withcindy]. (2018b, October 1). Why i only own 4 books 🧐 a chat on booktube consumerism. [Video]. *YouTube.* www.youtube.com/watch?v=82aYuS6SNrU

Pham, C. [@withcindy]. (2019a, April 2). Scarlett Johansson Asian Readathon. [Video]. *YouTube.* www.youtube.com/watch?v=ACvS_ckjIYw

Pham, C. [@withcindy]. (2019b, April 3). 🧧 Asian Readathon—May 2019. [Video]. *YouTube.* www.youtube.com/watch?v=ODMHgqIl52o

Pham, C. [@withcindy]. (2020a, January 7). The worst books I read in 2019 aka I wasted showering on this??? [Video]. *YouTube.* www.youtube.com/watch?v=L9t8BWltgsg

Pham, C. [@withcindy]. (2020b, April 30). This polygamist thriller book had the worst plot twists I've ever seen. . . . [Video]. *YouTube.* www.youtube.com/watch?v=wE5n7auyLs0

Pham, C. [@withcindy]. (2021, April 23). 2021 Asian readathon [Video]. *YouTube*. www.youtube.com/watch?v=wxxOc_rW8go&list=PLfDByaG5ml_7STlC-26AMZq1UMtU3HaRb

Pham, C. [@withcindy]. (2023, April 5). 2023 Asian readathon announcement [Video]. YouTube. https://www.youtube.com/watch?v=CtkQuu3K69w

Pham, C. (n.d.). *FAQs. With Cindy*. https://withcindy.carrd.co/#faq

Pianzola, F. (2021). *Digital social reading*. The MIT Press. https://wip.mitpress.mit.edu/digital-social-reading

Pressman, J. (2020). *Bookishness: Loving books in a digital age*. Columbia University Press.

Radway, J. A. (1991). *Reading the romance: Women, patriarchy, and popular literature*. University of North Carolina Press.

Rahim, Z. (2019, September 25). How the #bookstagram movement has changed the way fiction is marketed, reviewed and read. *The Independent*. www.independent.co.uk/arts-entertainment/books/bookstagram-fiction-books-instagram-publishing-influencers-a9110776.html

Ramdarshan Bold, M. (2019). Is "everyone welcome"?: Intersectionality, inclusion, and the extension of cultural hierarchies on Emma Watson's feminist book club, "Our shared shelf". *Participations: Journal of Audience and Reception Studies*, *16*(1). 441–472. www.participations.org/16-01-21-ramdarshan.pdf

Rasmussen, L. (2018). Parasocial interaction in the digital age: An examination of relationship building and the effectiveness of YouTube celebrities. *The Journal of Social Media in Society*, *7*(1), 280–294. www.thejsms.org/index.php/JSMS/article/view/364/167

Reddan, B. (2022). Social reading cultures on BookTube, Bookstagram, and BookTok. *Synergy*, *20*(1). https://slav.vic.edu.au/index.php/Synergy/article/view/597

Reese's Book Club. (2023). *Who we are*. https://reesesbookclub.com/

Regner, T. (2021). Crowdfunding a monthly income: An analysis of the membership platform Patreon. *Journal of Cultural Economics*, *45*(1), 133–142. https://doi.org/10.1007/s10824-020-09381

Rehberg Sedo, D. (Ed.). (2011). *Reading communities from salons to cyberspace*. Palgrave Macmillan. https://doi.org/10.1057/9780230308848

Riley, S., Evans, A., & Robson, M. (2022). *Postfeminism and body image*. Routledge.

Rodger, N. (2019). From bookshelf porn and shelfies to #bookfacefriday: How readers use Pinterest to promote their bookishness. *Participations: Journal of Audience and Reception Studies*, *16*(1), 473–495.

Roig-Vila, R., Romero-Guerra, H., & Rovira-Collado, J. (2021). BookTubers as multimodal reading influencers: An analysis of subscriber interactions. *Multimodal Technologies and Interaction*, *5*(7), 39. https://doi.org/10.3390/mti5070039

Rojek, C. (2001). *Celebrity*. Reaktion Books.

Rosenfield, K. (2017). The toxic drama of YA Twitter. *Vulture: New Yorker Magazine*. www.vulture.com/2017/08/the-toxic-drama-of-ya-twitter.html

Rutherford, L., Johanson, K., & Reddan, B. (2022a). *Cultural pathways to teen reading: Publishing industry challenges*. Teen Reading in the Digital Era—Deakin University. https://teenreading.net/publications-reports/

Rutherford, L., Johanson, K., & Reddan, B. (2022b). #Ownvoices, disruptive platforms, and reader reception in young adult publishing. *Publishing Research Quarterly, 38*, 573–585. https://doi.org/10.1007/s12109-022-09901-5

Rutherford, L., & Reddan, B. (2024). Finding a good read? Strategies Australian teenagers use to negotiate book recommendations. In C. E. Loh (Ed.), *The reading lives of teens*. Routledge.

Rutherford, L., Singleton, A., Reddan, B., Johanson, K., & Dezuanni, M. (2024). *Discovering a good read: Exploring book discovery and reading for pleasure among Australian teens*. Geelong: Deakin University.

Sampaio, I. S. V., & Costa, A. S. (2022). Brazilian BookTubers and the COVID-19 pandemic. *First Monday*. https://doi.org/10.5210/fm.v27i4.12579

Sanusi, T. (2022, April 28). The fight to amplify black stories on BookTok. *Huck*. www.huckmag.com/article/the-fight-to-amplify-black-stories-on-booktok

Schoonens, A. (forthcoming). *Exploring digital media ecologies of young adult fiction: Teen readers and online participatory cultures* [Doctoral dissertation, Queensland University of Technology].

Scolari, C. A., D. Fraticelli. & J. Tomasena. (2021). A Semio-discursive analysis of Spanish-speaking BookTubers. In S. Cunningham & D. Craig (Eds.), *Creator culture: An introduction to global social media entertainment* (pp. 75–95). New York University Press.

Seed, D. (n.d.). BookTok: The next chapter for booklovers. *Contact*. https://stories.uq.edu.au/contact-magazine/2023/booktok-the-next-chapter-for-booklovers/index.html

Senft, T. (2013). Microcelebrity and the branded self. In J. Hartley, J. Burgess, & A. Bruns (Eds.), *A companion to new media dynamics* (pp. 346–354). Wiley-Blackwell.

Senft, T. M., & Baym, N. K. (2015). What does the selfie say? Investigating a global phenomenon. *International Journal of Communication, 9*, 1588–1606.

Shapiro, L. (2018, February 19). Can you revise a book to make it more woke? *Vulture*. www.vulture.com/2018/02/keira-drake-the-continent.html

Silvera, A. (2017). *They both die at the end*. New York: Harper Teen.

Sorenson, K., & Mara, A. (2014). BookTubers as a networked knowledge community. In M. Limbu & B. Gurung (Eds), *Emerging pedagogies in the networked knowledge society: Practices integrating social media and globalization* (pp. 87–99). Information Science Reference.

Stein, L. (2015). *Millennial fandom: Television audiences in the transmedia age*. University of Iowa Press.

Stewart, S. (2021, September 3). How TikTok makes backlist books into bestsellers. *Publishers Weekly*. www.publishersweekly.com/pw/by-topic/industry-news/bookselling/article/87304-how-tiktok-makes-backlist-books-into-bestsellers.html

Sugg, Z. (2014). *Girl online*. Atria/Keywords Press.

Sutherland, K. [@km_sutherland]. (2020, July 21). 🐌 🐝 *COVER REVEAL! 🐝 🐌 Most of The Time, Author Life Involves Hour After Hour of Staring at a Screen*. [Photograph]. *Instagram*. www.instagram.com/p/CC3rOU3AoZu

Sutherland, K. [@krystal_sutherland]. (2021a, April 6). Are you ready to become a Hollow sister? Show me your #houseofhollow before and after! #booktok #reading. #fyp #foryou. [Video]. *TikTok*. www.tiktok.com/@krystal_sutherland/video/6948009387860577541

Sutherland, K. [@krystal_sutherland]. (2021b, April 9). Before and after Reneé Ahdieh's House of Hollow makeup tutorial ❤ #houseofhollow #reneeahdieh#thewrathandthedawn #fyp #foryou. [Video]. *TikTok*. www.tiktok.com/@krystal_sutherland/video/6948892289532005637

Sutherland, K. (2021c). *House of Hollow*. Penguin Books.

Thomas, B. (2020). *Literature and social media*. Routledge.

Thomas, B. (2021). The #bookstagram: Distributed reading in the social media age. *Language Sciences*, *84*, 1–10. https://doi.org/10.1016/j.langsci.2021.101358

Thumala Olave, M. A. (2020). Book love: A cultural sociological interpretation of the attachment to books. *Poetics*, *81*, 101440. https://doi.org/10.1016/j.poetic.2020.1010440

TikTok. (2022, September 20). *A new way to tap into the #BookTok community*. https://newsroom.tiktok.com/en-us/a-new-way-to-tap-into-the-booktok-community

Tolstopyat, N. (2018). BookTube, book clubs and the brave new world of publishing. *Satura*, *1*, 91–96. https://d-nb.info/1243779128/34

Tomasena, J. (2019). Negotiating collaborations: BookTubers, the publishing industry, and YouTube's ecosystem. *Social Media + Society*, *5*(4), 1–12. https://doi.org/10.1177/2056305119894004

TwotheFuture. (2022). The 'Fyre Festival' of Tiktok: Lightlark. Retrieved November 8 from https://www.youtube.com/watch?v=5fuZX-J8JMc

van Dijck, J. (2013). *The culture of connectivity: A critical history of social media*. Oxford Scholarship Online. https://doi.org/10.1093/acprof:oso/9780199970773.001.0001

Vanderhage, G. (2019). What is #ownvoices? *Brodart Books and Library Services*. www.brodartbooks.com/newsletter/posts-in-2019/what-is-ownvoices

Vélez, E. (2020, November 22). Found family: Literature that celebrates choice. *NYPL Blog*. www.nypl.org/blog/2020/12/09/found-family-literature-celebrates-families-choice

Velez, S. [@moongirlreads_]. (2020). Books that will make you sob. [Video]. *TikTok*. www.tiktok.com/@moongirlreads_/video/6858731924865797381

Veltman, C. (2022, October 24). Author Colleen Hoover went from tending cows to writing bestsellers. *National Public Radio*. www.npr.org/2022/10/24/1129175256/colleen-hoover-bestselling-author-releases-new-novel-it-starts-with-us

vivafalastinleen [@leen]. (2022). Little spiel on #booktropes inspired by @maebbi's recent vid!! [Video]. *Tiktok*. www.tiktok.com/@vivafalastinleen/video/7124040348392852779

Weigel, A. (2022, July 11). The trope-ification of YA fantasy and its marketing: On Alex Aster's "Lightlark". *Cleveland Review of Books*. www.clereviewofbooks.com/writing/alex-aster-lightlark-ya-fantasy

Wiederhold, B. K. (2022). BookTok made me do it: The evolution of reading. *Cyberpsychology, behavior, and social networking*, *25*(3), 157–158. https://doi.org/10.1089/CYBER.2022.29240.EDITORIAL

Williams, K. [@myfriendsarefiction]. (2022). Happy midweek! [Photograph]. *Instagram*. www.instagram.com/p/Cbc2Mf8LeY_/

Yoto Carnegies (2023). About the awards. https://yotocarnegies.co.uk/about-the-awards/

YouTube (2022, June 22). *Copyright transparency report*. https://storage.googleapis.com/transparencyreport/report-downloads/pdf-report-22_2022-1-1_2022-6-30_en_v1.pdf

Zappavigna, M., & Ross, A. S. (2022). Instagram and intermodal configurations of value: Ideology, aesthetics, and attitudinal stance in #avotoast. *Internet Pragmatics*, 5(2), 197–226. https://doi.org/10.1075/ip.00068.rap

Zhao, A. (2019). *Blood heir*. Delacorte Press.

Index

Note: Page numbers in *italics* indicate figures and numbers in **bold** indicate tables.

Abidin, C. 7, 17, 20, 27, 46, 80
ACOTAR series (Maas) 47, 68, 71
aesthetic practices: bookishness as aesthetic strategy 2, 3, 42; on Bookstagram 24–27, 42–45; BookTok videos 29; conduct of reading 6; properties of books 5; *see also* visual culture
algorithms, influence on book culture 22, 24–25, 27, 28
Archive of Our Own (AO3) 72
Asian Readathon 47–48
Aster, Alex 57–58, 68–72
attention economy 17, 27
authors: author as brand 63–66; changing roles of 45; innovative practices 37, 48–52, 81; relationships with readers 7, 17, 58–59, 68, 72
authors' methodology (this book) 8–10, 15; interview participants **15**, 30–31n1

Bean (Goodreads pseudonym) 70–71
Birke, D. 2, 19, 21, 47
Blood Heir (Zhao) 61
book blogs 6–7, 18; fan-run blogs 58
book clubs 3–5
book covers 38–42
Bookcraft YouTube series 50–51
book culture: bookish content on social media 14–16, 17–18, 22–23, 28, 30, 41–42, 79–80, 81–82; bookishness, performance of 2, 7, 8, 19, 37–38, 42; changes in 1–2; convergence with digital culture 5–8; emotional responses 27–30; literary discourse 6; literary sociability 6
book lovers 17–18, 19, 25, 36, 65; *see also* influencers
book marketing 2, 39, 57–58, 63, 65, 68–69, 74
Bookstagram: aesthetic labour 42–45; C. G. Drews (Paper Fury) 43–45, *44*; social dimensions of 14–15; visuality and bookishness 24–27
bookstore displays 27–28
BookTok 27–30; Colleen Hoover 64–66; *House of Hollow* cover 39–42; promotion of Aster's *Lightlark* 69–70; tropes, use of 72–73
BookTube: books as cultural capital 20–24; Cindy Pham 45–48; readathons 47–48
Boy Who Steals Houses, The (Drews) 44, 66–68

Index

branding: author as brand 63–66; on BookTube 20–24; celebrity book club identities 4–5
Burgess, J. 7, 21, 80

celebrity book club model 3–5
Chaudhary, Ayman 40–41
connection: interconnectedness, perceived 46–47, 50; social connection and social media platforms 16–20
consumerism 22; aspirational consumption 26; book buying vs. library use 46; bookstore #booktok displays 27–28; retail click-through purchase 59–60; sales of BookTok books 73
Continent, The (Drake) 61
COVID-19 pandemic 8, 63, 66

DAGR project (Australian Research Council) 8–9, 15, 79
De Leon, R. 72–73
digital culture: and changes in book culture 1–2; convergence with book culture 5–8
diversity: among BookTubers 22, 28; in publishing 48, 60, 66, 74
Dogcraft (YouTube series) 51
Drake, Keira 61
Drews, C. G. 38, 43–45, *44*, 63, 66–68; Patreon and crowdfunding 68
Driscoll, B. 3, 6, 7, 58, 61
Duyvis, Corrine 60

e-books 64, 66
Ellis, D. 22–23, 28
"everydayness" in content 17, 46

family of choice narratives 66
fanfiction 72
fantasy genre 26, 30, 68–69, 70, 71
Feeney, Catriona 23–24
Fehrle, J. 2, 19
Fisher, Tarryn 46
"flat lays" 25, 43–44, *44*
Fuller, D. 1, 2, 3, 6, 16, 19, 25, 81

gatekeeping functions 4, 57, 59
gender: gender-diverse audiences 63; gendered models of reading 4; trans/non-binary readers 61–63; women-centered stories 4–5
Gong, Chloe 69, 73
Goodreads 58; Aster's *Lightlark* 70–71; campaigns 61; "Our Shared Shelf" 4
Green, J. 7, 21, 80

Hall, R. M. 3, 4
hashtags 24–25, 28–29, 43, 72
Hello Sunshine media company 4–5
Hinojosa, Stacy 38, 48–52, 82
Honeybee (Silvey) 61–62
Hoover, Colleen 29, 63, 64–66
Hosein, Saajid 22
House for Lost Things, The (Drews) 45, 68
House of Hollow (Sutherland) 39–42, *41*

identities: brand identities 4; of influencers 17, 22, 25, 65; of marginalised groups 62, 66; performance of reading identities 2, 19–20, 37, 42–44
influencers: and content creation 79–80; personality of 17–18; and relational labour 7, 17, 23, 25, 42, 46, 63; stereotypes of 22; *see also* social media platforms
Instagram 24; visuality of 26, 80; *see also* Bookstagram; interconnectedness, perceived 46–47, 50
It Ends with Us (Hoover) 29, 66

Jacobs, Cait 40

Kardashian, Kim 4
Kindle e-readers 64
Kings of Nowhere, The (Drews) 45, 67

labour: aesthetic 42–45; affective 6, 7, 23, 25, 80; creative 43–45, 81; relational 7, 17, 23, 25, 42, 46, 63, 80; unpaid, in creating content 6
Lee, Elodie 30
Lee, Mireille 30
Let's Play videos 49–50, 52
LGBTQI+ issues/readers 61–63, 66–67
Lightlark (Aster) 57–58, 68–72
Litcraft project 50
"literacy sponsors" (Brandt) 4
Little Book Owl (YouTube channel) 23–24
Long, E. 1, 3
Lu, Marie 69

Maas, Sarah J. 47, 68, 71
makeup videos 41–42
marketing: book marketing 2, 39, 57–58, 63, 65, 68–69, 74; trope-based marketing 59, 74, 81
"Mary-Sue" 71, 73, 74n3
material objects: books as, and socio-material practices 37–38, 41; books fetishised as 24, 25–26, 43, 80
Messina, J. 69
Meta (formerly Facebook) 24
Miller, L. 65
Miller, Madeline 29
Minecraft (video game) 49–50
Murray, S. 2, 37, 58, 59

Nightbane (Aster) 72
non-readers, appeal to 65–66

Oprah's Book Club 3, 4
"Our Shared Shelf" (Goodreads) 4
#OwnVoices 60–63; C. G. Drews 66–68

Palfreyman, Jane 62
Paper Fury (C. G. Drews) 43–45, *44*, 66–68
parasocial friendships/interactions 7, 45, 46–47, 50–51, 58, 63–64, 68, 79–80, 81

Patreon (crowdfunding platform) 68
Penguin Random House 28
Penguin Teen 39, 40, 41
Pham, Cindy 21, 22, 38, 45–48
Pinterest 3, 67
practices, socio-cultural 36, 37–39, 41–42, 81
Pressman, J. 2, 42, 44

readathons (reader-marathons) 47–48
"readerly capital" 6
readers: demographic profiles 28; diverse communities 28; history of social reading 3–5; identity as 2, 7; reader labour 6, 58; reading as shared experience 1, 23–24; reading recommendation culture 16–17; relationships with authors 7, 17, 58–59, 68, 72; as tastemakers 58, 59–60, 74, 81
reading industry 1, 6, 7, 18, 52, 57–58, 60–61, 63, 70
Reese's Book Club (Witherspoon) 4–5
Rehberg Sedo, D. 1, 2, 3, 6, 16, 19, 25, 81
relational labour 7, 17, 23, 25, 42, 46, 63, 80
Rescue Tails series (Hinojosa) 51
Richard and Judy Book Club 3
Roach, Catherine 73
Rodger, N. 2–3, 42–43
romance genre 28, 30, 59, 70, 72–73
"romantasy" 30

self-publishing 45, 64–65
Senft, T. 17
Sentinels in the Deep Ocean (Hinojosa) 51
shelfie (book selfie) practices 5, 19, 37, 43–44, *44*
Silvera, Adam 69
Silvey, Craig 61–62
Slammed (Hoover) 64–65
social media platforms: attention economy 17; bookish content 14–16, 17–18, 22–23, 28, 30,

41–42, 79–80, 81–82; and changes in book culture 1–2; overview 14–16; paid content 18–19; participatory culture 21; and personal brands 21–22; practices 36–52; and reader tastes 59–60; and social connection 16–20; *see also* influencers
social model of reading 17
socio-cultural practices 36, 37–39, 41–42, 81
Spann, Shannon 39, 41
StacyPlays 48–52
Sugg, Zoe 4, 5, 49
Sutherland, Krystal 39–42, *41*

tastemakers: celebrity tastemakers 4; readers as 58, 59–60, 74, 81
text-based to visual culture shift 80
TikTok 27; TikTok Book Club 59; *see also* BookTok
trans/non-binary readers 61–63
trope-based marketing 59, 74, 81
tropes as communication tool 72–74
Twitter (X) campaigns 44, 60–61

van Dijck, J. 21
Velez, Selene 29
Veltman, C. 64
visual culture: Instagram 25–26; text-based to visual shift 80

Watson, Emma 4
Weigel, A. 71–72, 73
We Were Liars (Lockhart) 30, 66
Wild Rescuers series (Hinojosa) 51
Winfrey, Oprah 4
With Cindy (YouTube channel) 22, 45–48
Witherspoon, Reese 4–5
Wives, The (Fisher) 46–47
women-centered stories 4–5; *see also* gender

young adult (YA) fiction 5, 8, 21, 62; Aster's *Lightlark* 69–71; C. G. Drews 66–68
YouTube 20–21; *see also* BookTube

Zhao, Amélie Wen 61
Zoella Book Club 5

For Product Safety Concerns and Information please contact our EU representative GPSR@taylorandfrancis.com Taylor & Francis Verlag GmbH, Kaufingerstraße 24, 80331 München, Germany

Printed and bound by CPI Group (UK) Ltd, Croydon, CR0 4YY

23/07/2025

01922925-0006